EMBRACING ALL OF ME

IDENTITY-FOCUSED WRITING AND
SELF DISCOVERY FOR BISEXUAL,
PANSEXUAL, AND FLUID MEN

ROSS VICTORY

© 2025 by J. Ross Victory; Ross Victory; Embracing All of Me

All rights reserved. United States of America.

No part of this independent publication may be reproduced, distributed, or transmitted in any form or by any means, including photocopying, recording, or other electronic or mechanical methods, without the prior written permission of the publishing author, except in the case of brief quotations embodied in critical reviews and certain other noncommercial uses permitted solely by copyright law.

Written by J. Ross Victory
rossvictory.com

Cover design by William Sikora III

Contributors: Aaron H. Aceves, Dr. Tangela Roberts, Daniel Morales, Steven Spencer, Chongzheng Wei, Mpumelelo Zamokuhle Zulu, and Nicholas Cairns

Edited by Liz Saucedo, Wonderlist

Proofread by Danny Decillis

EMBRACING ALL OF ME

CONTENT NOTICE

This book is intended to provide inspiration and encourage and not intended to provide medical advice. Creative writing can be an effective tool in personal development, but it is not a substitute for science-based approaches for managing stress or PTSD related to one's identity. Exploration should be done at your pace and in a safe, nonjudgmental environment.

CONTENTS

Introduction	1
Pillars of Embracing All of Me	19
The Power of Storytelling	35
How Repressed Emotions Negatively Affect Physical Health	75
Storytelling As A Tool For Empowerment	91
Internal Inquiries	103
Types of Creative Writing	115
Storytelling Frameworks	139
An Anime & Superhero's Guide to Embracing Yourself	147
Developing Character Arcs	163
Writing as Rebellion Writing for Liberation	187
Horror As A Lens	203
Developing Your Writing Process	217
Strength Vs. Weakness Writing Assessment	231
Writer's Block	251
Building An All-Star Team	257
Final Thoughts	267
Closing Mantra	271

Sources	275
Acknowledgments	279
Other Books by the Author	281
Resources Page	283
Listen to the Podcast	285
Suggested Reading	287
About the Author	291

CHAPTER 1
INTRODUCTION

WHAT IS THIS BOOK AND WHY AM I WRITING IT?

"I write out of a desire for revenge against reality, to destroy forever the stuttering powerless child I once was, to gain the love and attention that silenced child never had, to allay the disappointment I still have with myself, to be something other than what I am. ... I write because I have faith in the possibility that I can eventually surprise myself."

– Francine du Plessix Gray,
I Write for Revenge Against Reality

I set out to memorialize my father, but in the process, I also confronted myself.

When I began writing my first book, *Views from the Cockpit*, my intention was to memorialize my late-father. The book began as a way to process my grief—a collection of reflections drawn from journal entries, an attempt to capture our relationship and the legacy he left behind.

But as I wrote, something deeper surfaced. Something that I ignored but refused to stay buried. What began as a father-son memoir became a mirror of sort, forcing me to confront questions I hadn't fully asked and answered of myself:

Introduction

Who am I beyond the roles I've been assigned? What parts of myself have I silenced, and why? What happens when the story I sought to tell doesn't fit into its own box?

Writing wasn't just a way to process and remember—it became an excavation. I found myself interrogating everything: our relationship, my masculinity, my faith, my interests, my place in the world, and my bisexuality. And in those candid conversations with myself, my sexuality kept pounding on the door, demanding to be let in, demanding to be seen and confronted on the page. But why?

Why at that moment? *Views* was supposed to be a father-son memoir, and it was. But I've learned that truth isn't something you can neatly compartmentalize. You can only get so far exposing one part of yourself while keeping another in the dark. Every thread of our being is connected, even the ones that are inconvenient.

When *Views* was published in 2019, I decided to leave out reflections on the intersection of masculinity and sexuality, choosing to focus only on my dad's influence on my masculinity.

For much of my life, I had struggled with the absence of representation—not just as a bi teenager but as a Black bisexual+ man raised in a non-affirming religious home. I knew what it meant to silence parts of myself for the sake of belonging. I knew what it meant to keep peace by sacrificing myself. For many years, I was comfortable with discomfort and just accepted the card I was dealt. I surely didn't know how to write about it!

Five years later, I returned to the manuscript of *Views* and finally added what had been waiting to be acknowledged—

something I wasn't ready to write before. This time, I was prepared to include my bisexuality within the context of loss, love, and reconciliation.

That revision wasn't only about making the initial book more compelling or expanding its themes to include LGBTQ issues. It mirrored something much bigger: the process of unfolding, the process of embracing all of me.

Day by day, I had been taking actions to reclaim authority over my life—to listen when my body had something to say, to honor my inner voice, to stop letting others' perceptions dictate my own.

The act of publishing the book itself was a first step in that process. And the revision wasn't just about *writing* the truth; it was about *living* it. It was about the choice to omit part of the story and the decision to come back to make it whole.

This book you are about to read, *Embracing All of Me*, is an invitation. An invitation to learn, write, reflect, challenge yourself, and ultimately, take ownership of your own story. It encourages you to revisit the moments that have subtly knocked and patiently tugged at you. It provides you with practical tools to write what must be written.

This book emerged from years of conversations, community gatherings, and my experience as a bi+ teenager to man. Those moments made me question:

"Where do I belong?"

"Am I even real?"

Introduction

I've asked these questions myself. I've heard them whispered, shouted, and agonized over in various spaces and in different voices by bi+ people from every background. From podcasts to in-person conversations. When I say bi+, I'm using an umbrella term to express all forms of attraction beyond a single gender. Some of us call ourselves bisexual, pansexual, omnisexual, hetero/homo-flexible, fluid, queer, or nothing at all.

While the title *Embracing All of Me* is intended to be warm and comforting, I want to be clear: embracing yourself in a world *like this* is an act of defiance.

Embracing yourself defies the systems and narratives that benefit from our fragmentation. In a society that constantly tells us which parts of ourselves are acceptable and which are not—race, gender, sexuality, body, class, ability, or belief— *choosing* to love and live as our full selves in the face of adversity is an act of rebellion. It disrupts and sparks liberation.

I also want to strip away all the propaganda and bullsh*t surrounding bisexual+ men and the LGBTQ+ community at large and state it plainly: systemic failures are costing lives in medical, social, and interpersonal ways.

Navigating this world as a bi+ person is like being locked out of your own house. Let's say you go to a locksmith, hoping they can help you open your door because you left the stove on. Instead, they tell you that you've gone to the wrong house and give you a different key, insisting it's the right one.

You know that key doesn't fit, yet they keep insisting. For some reason, you keep trying it—over and over—to prove them wrong.

Eventually, you start doubting yourself and wondering if you're the one who made a mistake.

Now, take it a step further. Imagine running into a fire station, panicked and desperate, because the house you're locked out of has caught fire from a stove. Rather than grabbing a hose, the firefighters check your blood pressure and dismiss your distress as "being dramatic."

Instead of walking away with a key that fits your house—or tools to put out the fire—you leave feeling helpless and humiliated. The door remains locked. The fire is still burning. Only now, you're left inhaling smoke, choking on someone else's disbelief, scrambling to fill buckets of water while trying to unlock into a door that was never broken.

This is what's happening in medical care, therapy, and social settings. And as a man, you're made to doubt your own reality, further fueling anxiety and isolation.

These failures aren't abstract hypothetical scenarios. In one instance, a man enrolled into therapy, questioning and obsessed about his bisexuality, and walked out believing he was a "confused gay man" because his therapist—a gay man—told him so. That session sent him into a spiral of alcoholism and suicidal ideation.

This isn't bullying or name-calling at recess. When a therapist, professor, or mentor—anyone with expertise, credentials, or cultural weight—labels a person's identity for them, it isn't an innocent mistake. It carries authority. It shapes self-perception.

And when that label is wrong, the damage isn't just personal. It ripples outward—into relationships, communities, and the broader cultural narratives about who is real and who isn't.

Bi+ women aren't faring any better. During an interview with *Embracing All of Me* contributor, Dr. Tangela Roberts, she shared research on the unfortunate reality that bisexual+ women are being screened and tested for cancers based on the gender of their partner. And while this book is written for us as bi+ men, this kind of erasure affects all of us—as another example of how systems fail those of us whose identities don't fit into binaries.

Dr. Roberts shared that medical systems frequently reduce complex sexual and gender identities into simple binary categories, leading to screening negligence. A bisexual+ woman with a female partner might be denied cervical cancer screening despite potentially having sexual histories involving penises. Missed diagnoses are potentially fatal to one's health and overall well-being. Social invisibilities and casual biases in the doctor's chair are linked to genuine health risks.

To quote Apollo 13: "Houston...we have a problem." A huge one!

This is the context I offer in this book—another resource to combat prejudice while taking control of what we can. It's designed to empower you with history and examples, while also giving you practical tools to form a cohesive, structured story.

As a former English as a Second Language teacher, I've worked with students from all walks of life—students of all ages learning to express themselves in a new language for the first time. My role wasn't only to teach English—it was to help people find their voice and reinforce that discovery process. This philosophy drives this book.

WHAT YOU'LL GAIN FROM EMBRACING ALL OF ME

With my experience as a published author, poet, music artist, songwriter, entrepreneur, former English teacher, and you're friendly neighborhood bisexual+ male, I've woven together insights and practical advice into a structured yet fluid format.

This book is intended to be both a creative writing guide and a self-discovery tool curated specifically for bi+ men. Whether you're a seasoned writer or a beginner who has never put pen to paper, *Embracing All of Me* will cover the following topics:

- **Self-Discovery & Identity-Focused Writing** – Explore how your experiences, identities, and emotions shape the stories you tell through writing exercises that help you connect with your truth.

- **Storytelling as a Tool for Empowerment** – Learn how writing can be used for self-advocacy and reclaiming narratives through various forms of storytelling like journaling, poetry, fiction, spoken word, or creative memoir.

- **Creative Writing Techniques & Structure** – Gain practical guidance on crafting compelling stories, from freewriting to character development. You'll also confront erasure and internalized shame by turning personal experiences into purpose and power.

- **Discipline, Prompts & Practice** – Access actionable exercises, conversation starters, and effective methods to help you stay focused and consistent to GET. IT. DONE!

- **Inspiration Through Community** – Discover the significance of connecting with others through shared stories, knowing you're not alone on this journey.

- **"You-Centered" Writing Practice** – Develop a sustainable writing routine to encourage your self-expression to become a lifelong tool and lighthouse for others.

Embracing All of Me is <u>not a purely instructional technical writing guide</u>. Storytelling is the most effective way to teach, mentor, and learn, so this book serves as a guide for beginners with examples of how writing can be transformative and help make abstract concepts more tangible.

However, this book is not all warm and cozy. I believe in love and light, spiritual connections, and all the lovey-dovey things that feel uplifting, but we also live in a world that demands resistance. To fight for something real, we must confront the stigma. We must confront ignorance. We also must be prepared. To get there, I'll take a grounded approach without being too harsh.

I encourage you to grab a notebook and a pencil for this! Along the way, you'll find personal stories, historical examples, quotes, creative techniques, tips, conversation starters, and reflection prompts to help you articulate your experiences in a real and practical way. To help with the complex theoretical chapters, a "Quick Action Guide" with a chapter summary and brief takeaways will follow the chapter.

At the end of the book, you'll find resources for writer's affirmations, further reading on identity and creativity, a link to the limited podcast, and a QR code to access the full list of prompts and reflection questions if you prefer to skip them as you read.

Lastly, I invite you to participate in the Writer's Challenge and share your work with your community while tagging #embracingallofme or #mystorymyterms.

IDENTITY-FOCUSED

At the heart of *Embracing All of Me* is **identity-focused writing,** a term I'll use often (maybe too much!) but that's the core of what we're doing. When I say "identity-focused writing," I mean storytelling that begins and ends with your own truth, the core of who you are, your origin story, and your principles and aspirations. In short, identity-focused places **you** at the center.

When we write from the core of who we are, we don't just tell a story; we establish an orbit that draws others into our gravity fields, inviting them to observe the world through our perspective.

By creating from what we know, what we've experienced, how we perceive things, and our progress, we give ourselves the opportunity to ask questions, think critically about our circumstances, and embrace our perspective with clarity.

Here's a visual comparing the richness of an identity-focused lens versus a so-called 'neutral' lens.

IDENTITY-FOCUSED

Captures experience, history, and meaning. Adds depth, emotion, and personal context

- ✓ Processes self-understanding
- ✓ Affirms identity against misconceptions
- ✓ Explores emotions and lived experiences
- ✓ Turns personal struggles into empowerment
- ✓ Bridges past and present identity
- ✓ Self advocates and pushes back against dominant narratives

- Might focus on stories that validate personal beliefs (e.g. citing negativity and ignoring positive examples)
- Might use emotionally charged language that makes it challenging for different perspectives to engage

NEUTRAL

Captures facts: who was there, the time, what objects were in the room, how many people entered, what they did, etc.

- ⊘ Instructional or informational
- ⊘ Detached storytelling
- ⊘ Entertainment-driven
- ⊘ Generalized topics

- Might claim neutrality but may omit certain voices
- Might cherry-pick research that only supports dominant narratives
- Might reinforce bias through framing, sensationalism and controversy

Credit: Ross Victory

Introduction

Some stories will stretch you, unsettle you, even contradict you in identity-focused spaces.

For example, I've heard it said—by someone who walked away from their LGBTQ identity and their community—that *God can't bless what God didn't create*, and that shedding their "sinful" queerness brought them closer to God and their purpose. On the surface, their identity-focused story or journey may be triggering if we feel it suggests our queerness is sinful.

But here's the thing, their truth is not my undoing. Their experience does not invalidate my truth and my experience, because I am whole. I remain a bisexual man who believes God puts us on a path of shedding narratives and labels that never fit—including the ones handed to us by organized religions.

How?

Because no one speaks for me.
And no one speaks for them.
No matter how loud we get.

Identity-focused storytelling isn't about debate, persuasion, or even objectivity. It's about *permission*—permission to take up space, to speak your name, and to share your perspective.

We're navigating an infinite number of expressions of identity and we're navigating *power*. When you write your story, you reclaim what they've tried to silence or erase. You can attempt to balance of scale of overrepresentation.

Identity-focused writing:

Recognizes That Life Experience Shapes Truth

- A black woman, an Asian man, a white mother, a bi+ man, an immigrant, and a disabled person in the same room are all experiencing the same physical reality, but their realities are not identical. For example, A bi+ or queer person may scan the room for signs of potential acceptance or rejection. An immigrant may be sensitive to cultural dynamics, language accents, and the feeling of belonging. A disabled person may assess accessibility and physical barriers.
- Their identities shape what they notice, how they move, what they fear, and what they feel safe expressing in the room.

Doesn't Force a Single "Neutral" Narrative

- If the room were described only from a "neutral" lens (for example, the security camera perspective), we wouldn't capture the richness of different lived experiences within the space. Without those experiences, we risk interpreting them inaccurately.
- Identity-focused writing elevates differences, making space for multiple truths by asking, "What is your experience in this room?" "What does it feel like to be in this room?"
- Identity-focused writing asserts your truth while inviting others to know what you're scanning for and what's at stake for you.

Introduction

Validates What Society Often Ignores

- The world centers dominant perspectives—straight, cis, able-bodied, white, etc.—as "neutral" or "universal."
- Identity-focused approaches say, "What you see, feel, and experience matters. And it deserves to be told." Identity-focused writing also acknowledges that readers' lives can be enhanced by learning about what else exists in the room that they cannot detect.

Asserts Presence in a Space That Might Try to Erase You

- Without identity-focused narratives, we only hear the perspective of the person who feels most comfortable in the room.
- When we intentionally create from an identity-focused space, we assert our presence and challenge the idea that only specific perspectives are worth documenting.

Scenario: A bi+ man looks back at his early childhood and teenage years and realizes he had strong feelings for both male and female friends but dismissed them at the time as something all kids had. Now, through journaling, he revisits those moments with clarity and acknowledges what he once ignored.

Think: Why is this identity-focused?

Scenario: A bi+ man in a long term, monogamous relationship with another man is frustrated by the stereotype that bisexual men are "confused" or "eventually going to pick a side." He uses an article, personal essay, or social media post to set the record straight.

Think: Why is this identity-focused?

Identity-focused writing is not trauma porn. It's not about proving our struggles just to be seen or playing in the oppression Olympics. Yes, some bi+ men face adverse health outcomes, invisibility, or misunderstanding—but that's not the whole story of us. Our writing must also make space for the fullness of our experiences: the joy, the love, the absurdity, the nonchalance, the quiet moments of self-acceptance. We are more than suffering and statistics. The key here is to cultivate awareness and empathy for others while giving ourselves permission to tell our truth, too—whether that truth is resilience, pleasure, heartache, or reclamation. It's Your Story. Your Terms.

Your goal is not to fix or change anything about your sexuality, your perception of what it means, or how you choose to navigate the world. Your goal is about being equipped to articulate yourself with purpose and clarity—one word at a time.

So, how do we put identity-focused writing into practice? Through five core pillars that will shape our journey.

Each chapter is guided by these five pillars:

1. Self-Discovery
2. Self-Advocacy & Empathy
3. Restoration
4. Embodiment
5. Aristotle's Poetics

These pillars form the foundation for our exploration of the writing process and turning personal stories into acts of liberation, and then acts of liberation into societal pushback.

Introduction

I don't intend to take a fully academic approach or be overly clinical, but in some cases, I'll use academic jargon to establish the foundation. For the heavier topics, I may use some light or suggestive humor to get us through.

You've made a decision to be here, and whether you want to pen a memoir, develop fictional characters, capture emotions in poetry, or simply look for an engaging read, my goal is to give you information, insight, and a personal action plan.

Your goal is not to fix or change anything about your sexuality, your perception of what it means, or how you choose to navigate the world. Your goal is about being equipped to articulate yourself with purpose and clarity—one word at a time.

When we do not honor our origin story, and we create from a place that isn't ours, the disconnection is evident. Readers can sense the cracks, the dissonance, and the emptiness in words that feel good but are unrooted in truth.

When you hold paradoxical identities that contrast with traditional expectations like bisexuality, it can be isolating. Revealing yourself may feel dangerous and who would want to subject themselves to more violence!? Violence in therapy or medical settings, rejection from family, or in some countries, physical violence, imprisonment, and death. It's as if every step we take needs to be justified, rationalized, and defended.

But when you intentionally write through an identity-focused lens, there's no expectation for you to get it right. The stakes are lower, and there's no expectation for your life or opinions to be neatly presented or well-researched because they are uniquely yours.

Sometimes the truth is inconvenient and disruptive to how someone else chooses to live or believe. But that doesn't make the truth any less true. Identity-focused writing is an invitation to share your narrative and tell your characters' stories from the place you know best.

It's an invitation to step forward, not step on.

To stand up, not stand over.

An invitation to raise your hand, not your fist.

This book is a tool. Add it to your war chest.

CHAPTER 2
PILLARS OF EMBRACING ALL OF ME

When I reflect on my career as an English teacher, higher education manager, advocate, author, songwriter, and artist, the five pillars mentioned earlier are the values I'd want to share with anyone closest to me: Self-Discovery, Self-Advocacy & Empathy, Restoration, Embodiment, and Aristotle's Poetics.

The pillars are not rigid rules but support beams to lift you up as you explore, ask questions about your humanity, and express yourself authentically, specifically through written form. If you are inspired by another creative avenue, follow that inspiration.

> *Think of Embracing All of Me as a house. Every house needs a strong foundation and reinforcement, and this house we're building is supported by these five pillars.*

Each pillar represents an element of embracing who you are by shifting your story into a tool for personal and collective empowerment and a weapon against doubt and shame. Let's examine each one.

1. SELF-DISCOVERY

This pillar focuses on reconnecting with your younger years by reflecting on your life experiences and exploring your origins. We are shaped by people and our surroundings, and how you discover may depend on the space you're in. Some cultures emphasize collectivism—the well-being of family, community, and social cohesion, while others prioritize individual desires above all else. The beauty of identity-focused writing is that it compels the author to stay true to their realities—both individual and collective truths. It's self-honest and holistic.

While we'll intentionally focus on bisexual+ perspectives and experiences, we know that our orientation does not exist outside of our race, gender, class, economic status, nationality, marital status, disability status, and the host of labels we embody, inherit, and claim.

This book centers on the experiences of bi+ men, but identity-focused writing is not exclusive to any group—it's the foundation of all authentic storytelling. For bi+ men, though, identity-led writing can mean finally confronting societal messages that attempt to define or erase this part of us.

Our orientation does not exist in isolation. Storytelling benefits us because the more stories we tell, the more space we carve out for bi+ men who have historically been overlooked and deemphasized. Storytelling for bi+ men is a stance against conformity. It's a protest.

As you'll see, self-discovery, like a storyline, isn't about arriving at a perfect answer or ending but about embracing the peaks and valleys of the journey, giving ourselves permission to evolve, and finding the courage to say, "This is my story. My terms."

Why it matters: Asking questions about yourself helps you understand your story honestly and be aware of your challenges and successes.

How to begin: Start by writing about a moment when you first questioned, "Who am I?" or had a sense of being alive.

2. SELF-ADVOCACY & EMPATHY

Once you begin to ask questions about yourself, the next step is becoming empowered to advocate for your needs, values, and perspective. Self-advocacy is about standing in your own corner—using your voice, setting boundaries, and most importantly, not expecting others to read your mind or know what you need.

This pillar also emphasizes empathy. By exploring your story, we begin to see how the experiences of others might intersect or diverge, understanding the suffering that comes from other forms of oppression. And yes, while we all have different levels of privilege and face various levels of oppression, suffering is a human-wide experience.

Writing becomes a tool for building empathy—for yourself and others—as you navigate a challenging, opinionated world. Erasure is heavy and exhausting. Writing gives us as bisexuals the power to self-advocate and directly confront narratives imposed on us.

Little did I know that I would begin a self-advocacy process after my father passed away in 2017. In 2017, I lost my dad to a mix of cancer, elder abuse, and financial fraud. That moment would serve as a catalyst, the tipping point where everything changed, for me to confront hard truths and to decide how to move forward.

His death, my brother's death, my parents' divorce after 30+ years forced me to reflect and ask myself questions about who I am and what legacy I want to leave. I had to consider what was within my control to get there. Confronting these questions was the only way to move forward. While this jolt of self-awareness stemmed from loss and grief, it also set the stage for evolution.

Pillars of Embracing All of Me

PAUSE & REFLECT

Think back to a moment that changed you. Maybe it was a single sentence—words that, once spoken, you knew would alter everything. Words that burned into your memory.

For example: "We're getting a divorce." "I'm bisexual+." "Your brother has cancer."

How did that moment shape your sense of self? What questions did it force you to ask? Have you ever told that story—entirely, in your own words? If not, what's stopping you?

Many of the questions I asked revolved around my identity as a man compared to my father. This led me to ask several questions: What does it mean to be a man? What does it mean to be a Black man in the United States? To be bisexual+? To be from Los Angeles? To have graduated from high school and university? What experiences and labels am I convicted by and why? Which identities do I prioritize, and is there a hierarchical relationship among them?

The more self-awareness you gain, the more you begin to understand the unique space you take up and its importance, no matter how small or grand.

Writing is one tool for working through grief, resentment, numbness, and anger and for claiming your story in a way that feels real and grounded.

Why it matters: Advocating for yourself helps dismantle internalized doubt and invites others to see you as you are on your terms at your own pace.

How to begin: Write about a time you explained an identity to someone. What did you say, and how did it feel? Consider a visible or invisible identity about yourself.

An example of a visible identity is when one of my former coworkers once asked another coworker who wore a hijab to work, "Why do you wear a scarf every day?" My coworker took a deep breath and explained, "Wearing the hijab is a choice and makes me feel empowered. It's about my relationship with my faith." This interaction demonstrates how a visible identity can be explained.

You can also consider an invisible identity like someone living with a chronic illness like fibromyalgia. Unlike the hijab, fibromyalgia isn't outwardly visible, yet causes pain and fatigue. A family member may think this person is always tired or lazy, not realizing there's something else happening beneath the surface.

If you've never had the chance to explain something about yourself, what would people be surprised to know?

3. RESTORATION

Restoration is about taking steps to heal from the harm that stigma and rejection have caused. This pillar focuses on nurturing ourselves, reimagining favorable outcomes, and rebuilding our self-worth. A few years ago, I came across a TikTok video of a teenager who filmed himself telling his mother he was bisexual+ to see what she would say.

In the video, he shares that he's revealing his sexuality in an effort to be more open with her. He also confesses he has difficulty communicating with her due to her reactions. The mother refers to him as deranged before suggesting he live with a friend outside of her house. While this is a heartbreaking example, many young people are carrying stories like this, often intensified by factors like social stigma, race, and class oppression.

While writing isn't the magic pill for bigotry, it allows you to name it and reclaim it. You're able to restore joy and curiosity and reframe your identity on your own terms.

For bi+ men, this might mean challenging binary scripts around dating and relationships or processing feelings around being kicked out, overlooked, or incorrectly labeled. Identity-focused writing is a way to process those messages and rewrite a narrative where our fluid attraction is a strength, not a red flag. Where we are livin' our life like it's golden and not a fiery pit in hell—a narrative where our origin shapes the story and its outcome.

Why it matters: Self-care and taking care of our body, mind, and emotions is crucial in a world that refuses to affirm us. When we feel good, we can build confidence, try new things, and set goals.

How to begin: Write about a negative belief you've held about yourself and reframe it into a statement of strength.

4. EMBODIMENT

Pursuing health and self-discovery are not just intellectual exercises—they are meant to be lived. Embodiment is the process of integrating what you've learned about yourself into your daily life. This part isn't necessarily about words, but it's about belief and faith in oneself through small steps.

This pillar asks: How do you show up as your true self in relationships, work, and community? What does it mean to embody self-pride, authenticity, and resilience in a world that often demands you shrink?

Think about it—the boss who's always telling you to "tone it down," the family dinner where you have to duck and dodge conversations about your identity or who you're dating to keep the peace, the dating app where you wonder if listing "bisexual+" will tank your chances for a date or send the wrong message.

These moments are demands to shrink, to contort yourself into something more "acceptable." But embodiment rejects that. Embodiment, thoughtfully, refuses to dilute yourself for anyone's comfort. Embodiment is believing your origin matters and has a purpose in the world, being comfortable in your skin, and displaying that comfort amid opposition.

For bi+ men, this may mean listing your orientation on a dating site or choosing to boldly show up in social spaces that have historically rejected or erased us—like LGBTQ+ events or even traditionally male forums for sports. Whether it's dating someone unexpected of you, proudly using a specific identifier, wearing or saying something that makes your identity apparent, or confidently rocking the boat, liberation is our birthright. The key is to point out that liberation and authenticity take on many forms, and sometimes, embodiment means knowing when, where, and how to be seen. Being able to properly read the room is key to embodiment.

Identity-focused writing can allow you to practice the confidence to express yourself on your own terms. Doing so reinforces, in your own words, why your story deserves to be seen and heard.

Why it matters: When you *"walk the walk"* you reinforce theoretical ideas into action and inspire others to do the same.

How to begin: Write down three ways you can embody your truth today—consider small actions, adjectives that describe you, or self-care practices that make you feel great.

5. REINFORCED BY ARISTOTLE'S POETICS

Aristotle's *Poetics* teaches that storytelling is fundamental to understanding ourselves and the world around us. For men like us, writing serves as a mirror when the world refuses to reflect us back. Identity-focused writing is our way of saying: we exist, we're complex, you may not get it, and that's ok because I do. It allows us to process and claim the truths at our own speed.

When your words exist on the page, they are undeniable proof: you are here, you are valid, and your story matters. His concepts of *mimesis* (imitation, representation, or mirroring life) and *catharsis* (emotional release of joy, grief, resentment, anger, or love) provide a historic and ancient framework for using writing and creativity as tools for personal transformation. Catharsis, the benefits of emotional release, is a key driver to include Aristotle's work as a pillar.

This pillar reinforces all the others, reminding us that writing is an art that reveals and restores. By using Aristotle's principles, we can give structure to our deeper truths and form a cohesive, commercially consumable, and connective story.

Why it matters: The act of writing is both a creative act and a form of self-advocacy.

How to begin: Reflect on what truths you are ready to express. When you think about the phrase "Embracing All of Me," what does it mean to you? How has the journey been? Where do you feel confident, and where do you need to improve?

Every word you write, every story you explore, adds another brick to this structure. By the time you finish this book, you will have built a home within yourself—a space where all of you are welcome.

*

One last point, the internet, bookstores, and Amazon are jam-packed with articles and opinions on how to write your first book. I know—it's a rabbit hole. The more you read, the more confused you get about where to begin. Should you self-publish? Should you aim for something authentic or something built to sell?

Writing isn't always easy, even in the time of AI. It takes intention, time, a keen eye, and sometimes resources we don't have. But it's a skill that can be developed.

I'm not a psychologist, spiritual guru, or literary genius. I used to wish I was, but I'm not. I'm an artist, a creator, an adventurer, a DIY-er, someone addicted to finishing for finishing's sake. I've quoted some psychologists, spiritual teachers, and authors, some of whom self-identified as bi or could be interpreted as bi, to underscore certain points to support the ideas I'm sharing here and to give visibility to paths that have been walked before you.

While writing is a deeply personal act, it can also be a professional, transactional one. Both are valid. Both matter.

As creators, we pour our souls into our work, and sometimes we're told it's not enough. We're told we need more social media followers to establish credibility or marketability. And while commercialism and capitalism are our context, your life isn't a transaction.

That's why I'm here—to remind you that writing can be therapeutic. Writing can help you understand yourself so deeply that you feel anchored no matter what the marketplace demands. And ironically, you may find an audience in the marketplace by sharing all of you.

"The soul that is within me no man can degrade."
-Frederick Douglass

CHAPTER 3
THE POWER OF STORYTELLING
BACKGROUND

Who Am I?

Civilizations across the world have asked this question, carving it into stone, painting it onto vast canvases, and etching it into the facades of sacred temples. From Auguste Rodin's *The Thinker*, a heroic-sized man frozen in contemplation in the heart of Paris, to the towering *moai* of Easter Island, standing as sentinels of forgotten histories, to the intricate corridors of Angkor Wat in Cambodia, where bas-reliefs tell stories of gods, kings, and the eternal struggle between chaos and order.

Humanity has long sought to capture identity in art and architecture. We have always written our stories into the landscapes we inhabit, layering meaning into brushstrokes and blueprints, hoping that in creation, we find recognition.

For many men, this journey of self-discovery can feel like wandering through an uncharted forest, where each path leads deeper into uncertainty rather than clarity.

For those of us who are bi+, this struggle is even sharper. Patriarchy insists that true masculine strength lies in solitude and silence, casting vulnerability as feminine and weak. But when your very existence defies rigid masculinity and sexuality, expression is essential for survival.

Conditioning has left many of us disconnected—from others, our bodies, our emotions, and our origin story. Not everyone is introspective, and reflection shouldn't be the sole measure of self-worth. But for some of us, questioning is not a choice. All we have are questions!

When you add the layer of complex attraction that falls outside the norm, such as a man attracted to men, and self-discovery can feel not only daunting but dangerous. It's no wonder many of us may choose to bury this part of ourselves (some for a lifetime) or at least deprioritize our sexuality.

> *Patriarchy insists that true masculine strength lies in solitude and silence, casting vulnerability as feminine and weak. But when your very existence defies rigid masculinity and sexuality, expression is essential for survival.*

Dr. bell hooks powerfully states in *The Will to Change*: "The first act of violence that the patriarchy demands of males is not violence toward women. Instead, patriarchy demands of all males that they engage in acts of self-mutilation, that they kill off the emotional parts of themselves."

This self-mutilation Dr. hooks describes is the fading spark in a boy's eyes as he becomes a man. It's the rejection of tenderness when it's most necessary, the stifling of tears before they can fall. Patriarchy doesn't just harm women—it targets us first. For bi+ men, as I mentioned, this burden is even heavier. The house is on fire! We navigate the same rigid expectations of masculinity as all men while also carrying the weight of our fluidity. These are attractions we did not choose—attractions that, by their nature, refuse to conform.

~~WHO AM I~~ I AM HERE

Neuropsychologist and author Julia DiGangi wrote in her Substack, "The opposite of uncertainty is identity. When you are frightened by uncertainty, this is your clearest signal to turn inward—a chance to decide: When those around me are shaking and systems seem to be crumbling, who will I believe I am?"

This internal investigation, this question, *"Who am I?"* offers us a rare and valuable proposition: the power to choose and the power to mold the answer. Through writing stories, we have a chance to curate and display our answers, defining not just our sexual orientation and making it fit within a binary world but also our values, boundaries, art, despair, and sense of self.

In this way, storytelling for bi+ men isn't just an opportunity for self-expression; it's an antidote to poisonous anti-bisexuality by shining a bright light directly at our voices and experiences. It's shifting the question of "Who am I?" to a proclamation, "I am here." We'll discuss "re-authoring" shortly to expand on how to do this.

If bronze represents the writing that any writer could express, and silver signifies the telling of common stories, then the purest gold captures moments only you have experienced and fool's gold glitter is worthless. But to write nothing at all? That's like leaving your treasure chest buried and empty. Unearth the gold that's already inside of you.

Storytelling can take many forms, each offering a different kind of opportunity. Certain experiences may not produce the best poem, but they could turn into a compelling short story. Some short stories are better envisioned as a song or a rap.

These forms are the canvas to explore key questions like: *Is my sexuality defined by what I do or by who I am? What type of relationships do I fantasize about? Who has caused me the most stress regarding this topic?*

Stories allow us to "live out" these answers in a creative way, free from others' judgments or limitations. Through stories, our bisexuality, fluidity, and all of society's projected labels can coexist, regardless of our relationship status, structure, or desires.

Journaling is a foundational writing method—a space to lay thoughts bare, unfiltered, and process emotions you might otherwise suppress. It also lets you archive your life and is a powerful way to identify patterns and opportunities.

Prose-style poetry can offer you a powerful way to explore emotions and situations, and even rewrite narratives that don't serve you. By blending the lyricism of poetry with the narrative nature of prose, it becomes possible to create vivid worlds where new perspectives emerge.

One particularly key technique is "re-authoring."

RE-AUTHORING

Re-authoring is a psychological practice rooted in narrative therapy that involves reshaping meaning and beliefs by challenging limiting societal narratives.

Consider the acronym LGBTQ+. Many believe it defines a group in opposition to heteronormativity, reinforcing the idea that queerness is "opposite" or "other." But what if we re-authored the acronym to the below:

L - **Liberation**
G - **Gratitude**
B - **Boldness**
T - **Truth-seeking**
Q - **Questions—ask them!**
+ more.

That sounds like a community I'd want to be in—how about you?

With re-authoring, you shift narratives from separation to empowerment and from opposition to offense. In this example, "LGBTQ+" stops being an identity marker for "them over them" and becomes an *invitation* around shared values. Values that many people, regardless of their orientation, can resonate with. For bisexual+ men, re-authoring offers us a unique tool to push back. And we can be clever and witty using it.

Here's a way to put this into practice:

Think about a time someone defined you incorrectly. Maybe a friend assumed you were straight, a co-worker thought you were gay, or a parent referred to you as confused. Rewrite that moment in your own words. What *should* have been said? What truth do you want to replace their version with? Here's an example before you try.

Original Scenario (What Actually Happened):

I worked at a popular electronics store in college, completely smitten with one of my coworkers. Let's call her Tamara. Tamara was smart, beautiful, funny, all the things, so I decided to shoot my shot—I sent her a MySpace message, asking if she'd like to go out and what she thought about me. I include a caveat that if she weren't interested, she could pretend like this message never occurred.

The next day at work, something felt... off. My coworkers watched me like they knew something I didn't. Finally, one of them pulled me aside.

"Hey, uh... Tamara was kinda confused about your message."

I felt my face heat up.

"Confused? Why?"

"Well... she thinks you're gay."

My stomach dropped. Now I had two problems:

1. I didn't want my coworkers to know I had put myself out there and been rejected.
2. I didn't know how to correct her assumption without also outing myself as bisexual.

It was a mess! So, I froze, laughed it off, mumbled something like *"Oh, Nah, that's not me,"* and changed the subject. The moment slipped away, even though it gnawed at me for days and years as an unforgettable reference point for things not to do at work.

The Moments Effects:

- I let <u>other people's assumptions define me</u> instead of speaking my truth.
- I <u>felt cornered</u> between having to justify my sexuality and unwanted visibility, so I avoided the conversation.
- I left the moment <u>feeling small</u>.

Re-Authored Scenario (How It Should Have Gone):

The next day at work, I caught the same smirks and side-eyes. Everyone was full of the same sh*t they're always full of. But this time, I was ready.

"Hey, so Tamara was kinda confused about your message," a coworker said.

But instead of fumbling, I shrugged.

"Yeah? I was pretty clear. What's confusing about asking someone on a date?"

They hesitated. Not the reaction they expected.

"Well... she thought you were gay."

I didn't flinch. "Oh, I'm bi..."

Silence. Processing. I could see the gears turning.

"I didn't know that."

"A lot of people don't." I grinned. "Now you do. Does Tamara want to date me or not?"

And just like that, I owned the moment. No shame. No awkward escape. My Story. My Terms.

The Moments Effects:

- I didn't let other people's assumptions define me.
- Instead of defending or hiding, I owned my bisexuality without justification.
- I walked away feeling in control, not erased.

TRY THIS

Try this! What's one moment where you felt like you had to shrink yourself? Write it down. Now, rewrite that moment as if you owned it.

Let's take it a step further and ask ourselves if severe heartbreak or loss can be re-authored. Can a parent who lost a child to a rare disease or a mother who miscarried ever tell their story as something more than hopelessness? Can survivors of generational traumas reframe history without dismissing violence? Can divorce, estrangement, or illness be rewritten as a story of resilience or meaning?

Re-authoring is *not* a substitute for justice, equity, policy change, or decency. It's not about gaslighting people into gratitude when their world is on fire.

Re-authoring *does* offer an alternative—a way to gently reshape and consider an alternative perspective over time, to hold both pain and power in the same container.

- ✓ **Reframing Imposed Narratives** - Re-authoring challenges cultural scripts and dominant stories.
- ✓ **Empowering Through Language** - Re-authoring uses parallels, metaphors, and redefinition to emphasize agency.
- ✓ **Affirming Complexity** - Re-authoring creates space for nuance, contradiction, and self-determination.

Re-authoring reminds us that the stories we tell about ourselves aren't set in stone—they evolve as we do. Re-authoring is an act of rebuilding. Just as the United States found a way forward after September 11, transforming the site of the fallen Twin Towers into something new and purposeful, we can also find a way through—reshaping our past into the foundation for what comes next.

Late scholar José Esteban Muñoz, a queer-identified Cuban American thinker, wrote and taught about the intersection of re-authoring and creativity. In his book *Disidentifications*, he described disidentification as a way for marginalized people, notably queer artists and performers of color, to engage with dominant culture—not by fully embracing it or outright rejecting it, but by twisting to fit into reality.

Think of a magician palming a coin. It looks like it disappeared, but really it's just somewhere unexpected. That's disidentification.

It's seeing yourself in stories that weren't written for you and saying, "F*ck it and f*ck them," and making those stories your own anyway.

Bisexual+ people, isn't this what we do all the time? We see characters who read as bi—EVERYTHING in the story signals they play for both sides—but the word is convieniently spoken. We sit through love stories, hookups, homoerotic nonsense, and everything in between that refuses to acknowledge anything outside of a binary, yet there is something we can discern.

Disidentification is what happens when a bi+ man experiences a hyper-masculine, emotionally charged friendship—the kind where the men fight, protect, and challenge each other with an intensity that borders on something more.

We detect queerness woven into it, even if the story doesn't say it out loud. It's catching the lingering glance, unspoken tension, the way bonds defy categorization, knowing that if the gender dynamics were flipped, the subtext would be the main text. *Say Amen if you know what I mean!*

It's when a woman has a male best friend she assumes is "one of the girls"—playfully pulling him into conversations about men and, heaven forbid, changing clothes in front of him, overlooking the way his attention lingers on her in a way that isn't fully platonic.

It's the jolt of recognition we feel when we see it play out on screen or in real life—the quiet identification with a dynamic that's been felt but never named out loud.

Take what exists, work around its exclusions, and reshape meaning in ways that validate our own experience.

Suffering breaks into our lives uninvited as well. Embracing all of yourself applies as deeply to tragedy—on a massive scale like slavery, genocide, or war, and on a personal scale like murder, loss, and interpersonal violence.

When tragedy enters your history, your lineage, your identity—*embracing all of you* means coexisting with grief, rage, joy, and love—without becoming debilitated or letting a single emotion become you. For those of us who've been there, or maybe in there now, it does feel debilitating and paralyzing when you understand the scale and impact of what has occurred.

For descendants of the enslaved, survivors of genocide, or those born from collective trauma, *embracing all of me* means confronting both inherited trauma and inherited resilience—because they are inseparable. We'll discuss more about inseparable experiences and identities in a bit.

Questions to consider:

- *What story will I tell about this loss?*
- *Will it be a story of defeat, or will it celebrate remembrance and endurance?*
- *Or perhaps the story is about the discovery of resilience?*

We clearly see this in Black culture, where African American artists, in particular, have turned their suffering into art—through blues, gospel, jazz, and hip-hop—transforming trauma into music, resistance, joy, and acts of preservation.

And what about when tragedy is deeply personal, when someone loses a parent or a loved one to something as unthinkable as murder? These experiences can never be rewritten or re-authored. I'm sharing these examples to show that embracing all of me can be claimed by anyone.

Questions to consider:

- *Is this story only about the violence?*
- *Is it about the love they gave, the memories they left, and how I chose to carry them forward?*

This is the heart of what we're doing in these pages. Not only the victories, the labels, or the identity politics. But the history—the hard questions and the truths that shape us, often without our consent.

PAUSE & REFLECT

What do you think about the concept of re-authoring?

Does reshaping a narrative give you more control over how you see yourself, or does it feel like an uphill battle against the expectations of others (or maybe even delusional)?

Re-author a label or identity that has been assigned to you. How can you redefine it in a way that aligns better with your truth?

I'll leave you with one last example ☺. I wrote a poem called *Braveheart*, where I reimagined a relationship between a mother and her faith. In the poem, the mother's faith in God helps her teach her son to love himself as he is. I was raised in a Black Christian home where the pastor preached sermons against the LGBTQ+ community as people chanted and cheered on. Writing this piece was a departure from the common narrative where religious belief conflicts with self-acceptance around anything that isn't straight.

In the poem, instead of the mother's faith being a <u>source of rejection</u>, it became a <u>foundation of empowerment</u>. Without his mother's faith, the son would not have been able to access self-love.

> **Original message = Source of rejection**
> **Re-authored message = Foundation of empowerment**

Through re-authoring, you can also reframe opposing ideas into harmony and affirmation. We will discuss more about journaling and poetry in future chapters!

A GLOBAL LEGACY OF FLUID ATTRACTION

As we set the stage for the work we came to do here, is there anything called bisexual+ specific history? Love and relationships are diverse and nuanced, existing across cultures and eras, far removed from Western, European-centered paradigms.

Historical records from ancient to medieval times—from East Asia to Africa and the Middle East—highlight individuals whose lives transcended binary understandings of attraction. These histories, preserved through art, literature, and mythology, remind us that language and narrative are vital for visibility and validation, along with how comfortable we feel in our skin.

Fluid expressions of love and identity have always been here, even when societies lacked the vocabulary to name them. For modern bi+ people, this history reveals a rich, affirmative legacy and an ever-present struggle for acknowledgment.

While the term "bisexuality," as we understand it today, began to appear in psychology and human behavior in the late 19th century (specifically from the 1880s–1890s), the experiences and identities it represents are ancient and unfortunately complicated over time by historians.

By tracing its evolution—from early occurrences of fluidity to modern advocacy efforts—we uncover untethered love in all its glory. People have always been out there loving who they love, experimenting, and going about their lives. Meanwhile, scholars are still in the group chat arguing.

GREECE

Ancient Greece is always a standout historical example of burning same-sex desires (5th-4th century BCE), where relationships between men were not only acknowledged but celebrated. Take the legendary, bisexual+ King of Macedonia, Alexander the Great, conqueror of empires and hearts of all genders.

His bond with army general Hephaestion ran so deep that when Hephaestion died, Alexander mourned like a man who had lost his soulmate—because, well, he had. Yet, Alexander also married Roxana, Stateira, and Parysatis, proving that his affections were as vast as the territories he claimed. In 2025, we refer to King Alex as bi. In the 4th century, who knows what label he might have been called?

Plato's *Symposium*, written around 385 BCE, explores the nature of love in ways that transcend binaries, reflecting a culture where attraction was multifaceted and matter-of-fact. But Greece was not unique. Fluid desire existed across continents, contexts, and religions. Let's bask in a few global examples.

JAPAN

In medieval Japan (12th-17th century CE), *shudo*, documented in texts of the era, described romantic and mentoring relationships between samurai. These bonds were celebrated as symbols of loyalty and personal growth, intertwining love with ideals of honor and masculinity.

ETHIOPIA, PERU & ITALY

In medieval Ethiopia, *ashtime*—effeminate men who blended gender expressions—held esteemed roles in courtly life, providing insight into the fluidity in their society.

Meanwhile, in pre-colonial Peru, the *quariarmi*—a term combining "qari" (man) and "warmi" (woman)—were shamans who embodied both masculine and feminine traits and were celebrated for their spiritual insight and diversity.

During Renaissance Italy (15th-17th century CE), *feminelli*, or gender-fluid individuals in Naples, found acceptance in both spiritual and celebratory spaces. Later in history, there was Hadrian, a bisexual+ Emperor who had a passionate relationship with Antinous, a young man from Greece. Hadrian was married to Empress Sabina for decades, and after Antinous died, the love was so deep that Hadrian named cities and temples in his honor! If that ain't love, what is it!?

INDIGENOUS PEOPLES

Indigenous North American cultures have long revered Two-Spirit individuals whose identities transcend binary norms. In many tribes, Two-Spirit people held special roles as healers, storytellers, matchmakers, or ceremonial leaders, seen as embodying both masculine and feminine spirits.

For example:

- The **Lakota** people recognized *winkté*, a term for male-bodied individuals who lived and expressed themselves in traditionally feminine ways.
- The **Navajo** (Diné) have the concept of *nadleehi*, referring to individuals who can change between genders and are respected as mediators and caregivers in the community.

These roles, predating European colonization, show that fluid identities have always existed and were respected and valued in societies that saw them not as deviations but as parts of the whole.

So, if we're being real for a second—asking Alexander the Great or a samurai practicing *shudo* how they identified 2,000 years ago would be nothing short of ridiculous. Most pre-modern people didn't label sexuality and gender the way we do. In some cases, they knew better and just drew the cave painting of people having sex and called it a day.

People loved, desired, connected, f*cked, and took on domestic roles without politics attached. Unless they documented their own lives—or someone else wrote about them—their truth would be lost to history. Many historical figures that historians now labeled as "gay," "bisexual," "trans," "non-binary," or even "straight" actually had diverse relationships, appearances, and roles. However, records favor the perspectives (and budgets) of whoever's writing them.

That's power indifference, and in 2025, that's a problem—hence the motivation for this book.

Everyone exists and people don't just disappear. Not only in matters of sexuality or self identification, but in broader historical erasures, particularly of non-male conquerors, unexpected thriving communities, and more.

Take the Kingdom of Dahomey, a West African empire (1600s–1800s) with an elite all-female military force, the Agojie, who inspired *The Woman King* and the Dora Milaje in *Black Panther*. Or the Mosuo people of China, where women have led a matrilineal, female-driven society for centuries, rejecting traditional marriage and passing land through mothers.

Ancient history is full of surprises—like the lost city of Cahokia, a massive, advanced Indigenous metropolis near present-day St. Louis. To most, it looks like just another hill, perfect for a workout. In reality, it was the largest and most influential ancient megacity north of Mexico pre-Colombus.

These societies didn't vanish. So, the real question is who benefits and who determines which narratives are elevated and which are diminished if not erased.

*

Egyptians offered their love poems to the future, inscribing their worlds onto the rock, leather, plaster-coated wooden tablets, and earthenware vessels—offering up raw, unapologetic interpretations of gods, death, society, and technology. And they never ever forgot the sex.

So let's be like the Egyptians, shall we?

History has answered the question of bisexuality's legitimacy. Why do governments, medical institutions, mainstream media, your favorite celebrity, YouTubers, and parts of the LGBTQ+ community still act like it's something to be debated?

It's always been about winners and losers. Those who control the narrative hold the key to the burning house.

When you know your history, you see past the hoopla and bullsh*t. You stand taller. You're more magnetic. Because instead of waiting for someone to hand you the right key—you kick the damn door down to save what's yours.

PAUSE & REFLECT

When someone misrepresents a story, yours or someone else's, what do you think their motive is? Is it ignorance, power, fear, or something else? Can stories ever be preserved accurately?

What are your thoughts about teaching queer history? Does it make a difference in how a modern LGBTQ+ person or child views themselves?

If no one wrote about you—your identity, experiences, relationships—how would future generations interpret your life? Would they get it right or wrong, and why?

MODERN TIMES

In modern times, artists and writers continue to capture fluid desire in their work. William Shakespeare's sonnets express deep affection for both men and women, while Walt Whitman's *Leaves of Grass* celebrates love that transcends gender. These works remind us that bisexuality is neither a "woke" concept nor uniquely European—it is a universal, discernable aspect of human expression and well-preserved through art and literature.

The modern bisexual+ movement emerged in the late 20th century, propelled by advocates like Brenda Howard, the Mother of Pride, who were determined to combat erasure within both LGBTQ+ and mainstream spaces. In the 1980s, the North American Conference on Bisexuality became one of the first professional organizations dedicated to the community.

By the 1990s, BiNet USA created a national platform for activism, while Michael Page's bisexual+ flag (1998) became a unifying symbol of pride. The establishment of Bisexual+ Visibility Day in 1999 further solidified the movement, celebrating bi+ resilience and contributions every September 23.

Despite these advances, forces like patriarchy, racism, and classism persist and compound the invisibility of bi+ people. Patriarchy enforces rigid gender roles, making bisexual+ men soft and gay and bisexual+ women subservient and untrustworthy.

For bi+ men of color, racism adds another layer of cruelty, as we are required to navigate cultural expectations of masculinity and erasure within a predominantly white-centered, gay-focused LGBTQ+ movement. On the surface, the choice is between two options: do you choose the comfort of your racial group and potential hostility regarding your sexuality, or do you choose the comfort of a sexuality-based community and face hostility toward your race?

One's class further deepens the divide. Those from working-class backgrounds or those who are housing insecure with economically marginalized circumstances lack access to platforms, resources like this book, and representation that illuminate their perspectives.

Trying to survive in fight, flight, and freeze mode while also being told to "man up," or "be strong" leaves little to no room for reflection or emotional expression, forcing many folks who could benefit from a bit of introspection to suppress parts of themselves simply to make it through the day. How does one pursue self-advocacy or embodiment when they are hungry and in danger? They don't.

These compounded forces push men like us to the fringes, leaving our stories misunderstood, excluded, and caricatured in media, film, and social media despite being part of humanity's narrative for millennia.

The goal for writers and creators like me is to make this information and history accessible and digestible, ensuring it gets into the hands of people who can benefit the most. But I need your help.

As you explore, consider not only your personal narrative but also the broader context of what you represent. Your unique experiences are, in fact, entries in a global and historical record book of similarly drawn paths.

While history provides a lens to understand the persistence of fluid identities, identity itself is multifaceted, shaped by the interplay of self-perception, social influences, and inherited circumstances.

And unfortunately, we can't just write love poems like the Egyptians or paint naked people on the wall (I suppose we can, but you get what I mean). Our identities become weapons for the will of politicians and corporations to conquer, confuse, and divide. We are demographics of potential revenue. The compounding nature of these forces and the barriers they create make embracing all of oneself feel like a pipe dream.

DO LABELS TELL THE FULL STORY?

I published this book in 2025, a time when identity politics elects presidents but also forms communities. It raises the question: what is identity? Is it something assigned to us, something we choose for ourselves, a combination of both, or maybe neither? Is identity created through our actions or what we believe?

What if we also ask what *isn't* identity?

For psychologists, sociologists, and philosophers, the answers can vary, but for writers, the key lies in how identity is shaped and expressed by the self, society, and our circumstances.

Conversations about identity are not just academic or political bait—they're invitations to understand our characters, real or fictional, in deeper ways to keep readers engaged. As you read along, you'll find exercises to help you apply these concepts into action. First, I would like to give some background on the idea of identity.

Sociologists like Henri Tajfel suggest that identity labels are shaped through group memberships like high school cliques—

jocks, nerds, hot gurlz, hot boyz, band geeks, and other terms. For example, being part of a cultural group, religion, or professional community influences how people see themselves and are seen by others. These identity labels are sustained and reinforced through social norms and discourse. Such labels can empower or restrict.

Existentialists like Sartre have suggested that identity is fluid and something we actively construct through our actions and choices, a blend of choice and circumstance.

Psychologist Dan McAdams refers to identity as a "life story" that provides coherence to our personal and social identities. Coherence can be understood as aligning your inner world with the outer world.

Some suggest that transition or crisis can jolt awareness of identity. Transitions (like parenthood, moving to a new country, graduation, or aging) force people to become aware of and reassess their labels and roles.

> *Note: If these theories feel abstract at first, don't worry—think of them as tools to sharpen your storytelling and your ability to develop characters or understand more about yourself. Each concept will later be paired with an example, prompt, or conversation starter so you can see how to apply it to your writing.*

IDENTITY CAKE

When I describe identity-focused writing, I want you to think of your favorite cake. But a layered cake. And not just a simple layered cake like, say, butter toffee pecan or strawberry vanilla, but a cake with so many damn layers that every time you cut deeper, you discover a new layer—jam, cream, frosting!

There's a catch, of course. You don't know how many layers there are from the icing covering the cake. And everyone is essentially their own "cake."

As I use this term identity-focused writing, I am referring to the following key "layers" or elements:

- **Who you are** (self-perception, intrinsic motivations)
- **How others see you** (social context, how others perceive you)
- **Who you want to be** (aspirations)
- **Inherited reality** (name, birthplace, parents)

To ground these concepts in practical terms, let's explore the various dimensions of identity and how they shape both real and fictional lives.

Every human is a summation of parts "layers under icing." As you read the list, consider the labels you use in each category. Also consider which elements are visible and invisible about you.

Personal

- Personality traits (e.g., introverted, adventurous, empathetic).
- Hobbies and interests (e.g., artist, book lover, athlete).

Cultural

- Ethnicity, nationality, and heritage (e.g., Latinx, Han Chinese, Navajo, Celtic, African diaspora).
- Traditions and practices shaped by cultural context.

Social

- Gender and sexual orientation (e.g., woman, man, nonbinary, LGBTQIA+).
- Class or socioeconomic status (e.g., unhoused, middle class, wealthy).

Professional

- Career or role (e.g., teacher, engineer, entrepreneur, farmer, unemployed).
- Skills and expertise (e.g., leader, creative, problem-solver).

Familial

- Family roles (e.g., parent, sibling, caregiver).
- Relationship status (e.g., spouse, divorced, partner, single, polyamorous).

Spiritual

- Religious affiliation (e.g., Christian, Muslim, Hindu, atheist).
- Spiritual beliefs (e.g., mindfulness practitioner, nature worshiper).

Political or Ideological

- Political affiliation or beliefs (e.g., progressive, conservative, libertarian).
- Advocacy or causes (e.g., environmentalist, feminist, human rights advocate).

Physical

- Body and ability (e.g., disabled, tall, curvy, fat, muscular).
- Health-related experiences (e.g., cancer survivor, chronic illness warrior). *Medical diagnoses are not identities*

Community

- Group memberships (e.g., sorority member, online gamer, local club).
- National identity (e.g., Southerner, urbanite, islander, refugee).

Temporal

- Life stage and age (e.g., teenager, millennial, elder).
- Era identification (e.g., 90s kid, Gen Z, Baby Boomer).

The cake has a lot of layers, right? Each category and label also comes with norms, culture, and expectations of what it means to occupy a space in that group. So, you can imagine how much opportunity there is for conflict as well as the treasure of knowledge and experience each person embodies with their specific "cake."

When we write about identity—our own or that of a fictional character's—we're inviting others to see, feel, and connect in the orbit of that life, seen and unseen factors. When creating characters, we should consider how they show up in each of the above areas as an exercise for comprehensive understanding. We can also reflect on how we show up in each of the above areas to evaluate and analyze how our world is built.

Identity and modern labels evoke strong feelings and start wars. I suppose they always have. Yet how can one identity or one label ever tell the full story? While I'm a bisexual+ Black man from the United States, I'm also a brother, friend, and uncle. I'm also a millennial, agnostic, and independent. But I'm so much more. I'm *becoming* so much more. I want a label that encourages me to Be More.

Like an iceberg, what's below the surface is always more than what you see. When a bi+ man writes from one identity, he writes from them all—our sexuality, our masculinity, our culture, our upbringing—all intertwined. Identity-focused writing helps us see how these layers are connected rather than letting others define them for us.

Legal scholar Kenji Yoshino introduced the concept of "covering" in his book *Covering: The Hidden Assault on Our Civil Rights*. Covering is when marginalized people minimize parts of their identity to fit in. Unlike passing, which is total concealment, covering lets someone remain technically "visible" but only on terms society finds acceptable. Yoshino broadly focuses on LGBTQ+ individuals, particularly how gay men and lesbians feel pressured to minimize their queerness.

But what about bi+ men?

The topic of bisexuality, concealment, and covering is rarely discussed publicly and rarely explored within community spaces. But go to YouTube or TikTok, and you'll find that people have *a lot* to say about bi+ men. The conversations—often not led by us—are riddled with assumptions, misunderstandings, and outright hostility.

Concealment and covering are survival strategies in a world at war with us.

Growing up, my mom once told me, "Ross, sometimes the world is at war with you, and you won't even know." I didn't understand what she meant—until I did.

And while she was speaking to me as her Black son, those words revealed why covering is not just about identity—it's about safety. Socially. At work. With the police. It also revealed that the state of being bisexual+ in the United States, specifically Los Angeles, are very different from countries that have outlawed identifying as LGBTQ.

I remember calling my mom at work and noticing how different she sounded compared to how she spoke at home. It was still my mom, but there was something more enhanced and polished about her tone. Her voice had a higher pitch, and she enunciated ev-er-y syl-la-ble. At that time, I just thought she was using her "work voice." I didn't realize that, as a Black woman in an all-male, all-white work environment, she had to cover—to code-switch—to be accepted.

We all learn this lesson in different ways.

It's so easy to critique a community from the outside, to scoff at bi+ men who choose not to disclose their orientation and make assumptions about our motives. But the real question isn't why a bi+ man covers—it's why the world makes it a requirement.

- ☞ Why would a man actively choose to conceal his sexuality?
- ☞ Why does honesty feel like a risk, not a relief?
- ☞ Why do we rarely hear about the bi+ community at all?

No one asks these questions enough. A Bi+ man who chooses silence or keeps his identity private are viewed as deceptive instead of cautious and self-preserving. We're seen as a walking danger to women's health. How ironic that people so easily slap on lazy stereotypes while still demanding those men "open up," but "not in *that* way!"

For bi+ men, covering is a negotiation of risk.

- ☞ Visible enough to be valid.
- ☞ Not too visible that it disrupts expectations.
- ☞ Not too ambiguous as to raise suspicion

Imagine this: It's Christmas dinner. A closeted bi+ man sits at the table, passing the mashed potatoes, when his sister cracks a joke—something about social media not being able to trust bisexual men, about how they're probably having all kinds of unsafe sex, about how they're really just gay or straight and afraid to admit it.

Laughter explodes at the table. His cousins chuckle. His uncle smirks. His mother doesn't object.

And even though it stings, mildly devastating, he doesn't flinch. He doesn't challenge his sister. Instead, he does something worse.

He plays into it. "I mean, do bi guys even exist?" he jokes, offering up his own identity as collateral.

This is covering in its rawest form—beyond silence, but participation. The easiest way to survive this moment is to sacrifice himself.

Have you ever been in a situation like this?

Imagine this: A bi+ man joins his gay friends for a night out at a popular queer bar. The energy is electric—drag queens are performing, the music is loud, and he feels at home in a way he never did in a sports bar. But then, dating comes up and someone in the group makes an offhanded joke, "Ugh, I could never date a bi guy again. Too much drama."

His stomach tightens. He was about to mention that he went on a date with a woman last week—but now, he hesitates. He nods along as his friends complain about "wishy-washy bi men that always end up with families."

Later, someone asks, "So, when did you know you were gay?"

He just shrugs and says, "Oh, you know...it took me a while to figure things out like everyone else."

Have you ever been in a situation like this?

I believe that *most* bi+ people have an innate sensor for homophobia and anti-bisexuality—a subconscious radar scanning every space, every conversation, calculating how much truth is safe to reveal. Calculating how dodgy we should be with the true pronouns of our partners.

Asking why bi+ men cover is just the first step. Answering it is the real work.

And the best way to do that?

If society refuses to write a space for us, we must carve it out. We have to muster enough strength against all odds to show them why, tell them why—before they decide for us.

Let's do more than just ask why.

Let's demand they show respect for our name. And let's make damn sure they can read it clearly.

PAUSE & REFLECT

In your writing, how might a character experience tension from covering and concealing their sexuality or any other identity in a social setting? How does it shape their interactions?

As you reflect on categories, identities, and labels, remember that you're more than what the world calls you at that time. And what is representation without liberation? What is the purpose of taking on all the history and propaganda of a label unless more freedom is the goal?

Whether you're crafting a character or reflecting on your own life, exploring layers of the cake or what's under the iceberg can provide a rich adventure full of twists and turns. Just imagine how a character's cultural background might inform their values while their familial identity adds emotional stakes to their choices. Maybe you've experienced friction that could also inspire one of your characters.

Our identities define us and our characters, but vulnerability and connection are what make the audience care. Stories of struggle, failure, and evolution through experiences of love, loss, and belonging are shared across all identities.

☞ Love. Loss. Belonging.

While we don't choose our name, birthplace, parents, or how society treats us, we do have the power to choose how we respond to oppression and suffering, even if it's just a prayer for relief or adjusting our perspective. Identity-focused writing belongs to all of us.

My Story. My Terms.

Select one:

Prompt: Write about a time when someone misunderstood or misjudged your identity. How did it feel? How would you rewrite that moment to reclaim your wholeness?

Prompt: Choose one dimension of your identity inspired by the list above and describe how it shows up in your everyday life. What do people get wrong? What do people get right?

Dig Deeper: Write a short scene where a character struggles with the clash between two dimensions of their identity (e.g., cultural vs. professional, familial vs. personal). How does the conflict resolve, or does it?

Dig Even Deeper: Choose one inherited identity label (e.g., birthplace, ethnicity, or name) and imagine how your character might reshape its meaning in their life.

SELF-DISCOVERY FREE WRITING EXERCISES

Exploring Identity:

- What is one of your sparks (passions, interests, talents)? When did you discover or feel this spark?
- Create a timeline of key moments in your identity development.
- When did you know you were attracted to multiple genders? Describe your first crush(es). Do you experience romantic and sexual attraction similarly or not at all?

Connecting to History:

- How can historical perspectives on gender and sexual fluidity enhance your understanding of your story?
- What historical figure or perspective would you be interested in learning more about?

Looking Ahead:

- What would you recommend your children to do or not to do?
- Who or what brings you peace and the greatest sense of calm?

CHAPTER 4

HOW REPRESSED EMOTIONS NEGATIVELY AFFECT PHYSICAL HEALTH

SETTING THE STAGE

Repressed emotions and unaddressed trauma can have profound effects on physical health. As children, we encounter emotions we can't fully process, and as we age, we may normalize these feelings without realizing their impact.

According to the Centers for Disease Control and Prevention (CDC), nearly 61% of adults report experiencing at least one adverse childhood experience (ACE), with 16% reporting four or more. These experiences—categorized as abuse, neglect, and household dysfunction—can disrupt brain development, impair emotional regulation, and lead to challenges like heightened stress responses, difficulty forming relationships, and low self-esteem.

My intention in sharing this is to acknowledge the experiences that may have shaped us and to remind us that we are not the problem—the problem itself is the problem. By naming and contextualizing our struggles and using art to express them, we can move from the passenger seat to the driver's seat of our own lives.

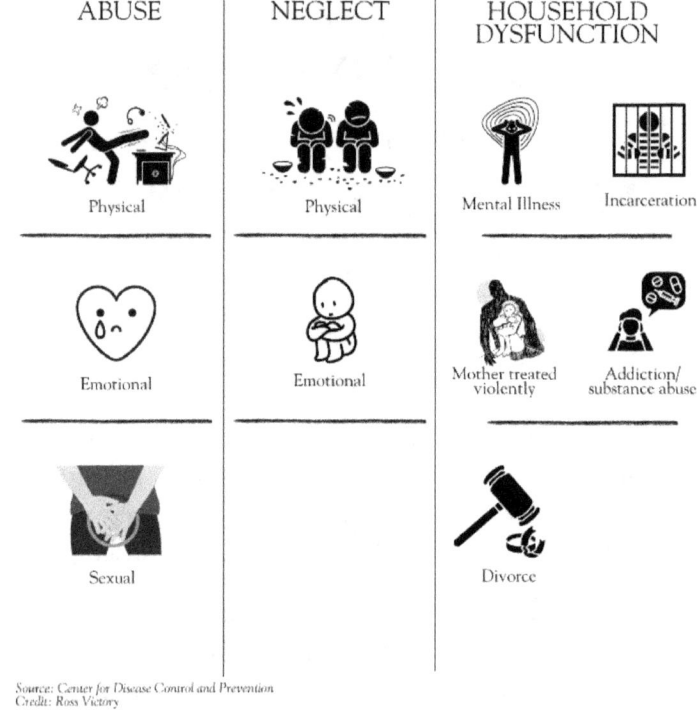

Source: Center for Disease Control and Prevention
Credit: Ross Victory

ACEs have been linked to a range of adult health conditions, including headaches, anxiety, depression, and even heart disease. For bi+ men, these challenges are, of course, compounded by societal pressures like homophobia, racism, and sexism, layered on top of expectations around masculinity.

According to Substance Abuse and Mental Health Services Administration (SAMHSA), 70% of adults in the U.S. have experienced at least one traumatic event in their lifetime. LGBTQ+ individuals, per usual, are at an even greater risk for trauma due to societal stigma and violence. In fact, 39% of bisexual+ adults report mental health issues, compared to 26% of heterosexual adults (Psychology Today).

It's important to note that an ACE score does not capture the full picture of someone's life. It doesn't account for love, affirmation, and complex positive experiences that can coexist alongside adversity.

*

Research published in *Psychological Science* (2013) found that individuals who wrote about difficult experiences in a structured narrative style experienced reduced symptoms of depression and improved emotional clarity over time.

Repressed emotions and adverse experiences often manifest as our "inner child"—what psychologist Carl Jung describes as an "archetype" that embodies our innocence, creativity, and emotional vulnerabilities developed during our formidable years, which we'll expand upon later. Like any child, if ignored for too long, this inner child can become unruly and demanding, creating challenges that prevent us from being comfortable in our adult skin.

Perhaps you've seen this play out in real life: someone you know suddenly makes a drastic life change that seems "out of the blue" or has an emotional breakdown or angry outburst that leaves those around them in shock. But was it really "out of the blue," or were they carrying invisible heavy burdens of unaddressed experiences for years, eventually reaching a breaking point?

This happened to me during my time in Seoul, South Korea, where I had moved to teach English. One evening, as I walked to the subway, my chest suddenly felt like it was caving in. I thought I was having a heart attack. Struggling for breath, I fell down a flight of stairs and ended up in the hospital despite no obvious injuries. The doctors assured me nothing was physically wrong and told me to "calm down and breathe."

To an observer, it might have seemed like this moment came out of nowhere, but in truth, I had been ignoring my body's signals for a long time. I had normalized physical symptoms of stress without realizing they were warning signs.

Under the surface, I wasn't just homesick and stressed from living abroad. I was coping with my parents' 30-year divorce and my brother's Stage 4 brain cancer diagnosis while still coming to terms with my sexuality—a tall order for anyone!

Many of our emotional triggers can be traced back to childhood experiences. Psychologists note that our inner child reacts to perceived threats rooted in unhealed wounds, leading to patterns of hyper-vigilance, avoidance, or emotional shutdown.

PAUSE & REFLECT

Are there physical sensations—headaches, tension, fatigue—that you've come to accept as "normal" but might be signs of unprocessed emotions or stress? When did they start, and what might they be trying to tell you?

- Avoidance Behavior
- Hypervigilance
- Obsessive Thoughts and Compulsive Behaviors
- Subconscious Coping
- Changes in Sleep Patterns
- Subtle Body Language Changes
- Mood Swings and Irritability

(Examples of physical sensations and behaviors to be aware of)

The added layer of navigating same-sex attraction in a society that polices the way men walk, talk, sit, eat, think, bend, and bathe compounds these challenges. Emotional vulnerability is generally equated with weakness, and many men struggle to justify their sense of masculinity when faced with genuine feminine-deemed qualities like same-sex attractions or non-traditional hobbies and interests like ballet, makeup, or caregiving.

The goal of the day, for many men, is not to be called gay or suspected to be gay so as to avoid being undesirable. And to your surprise, the social goal of many bi+ and gay men is also to avoid being called or suspected to be gay and also avoid being undesirable (let's save that for another book!). This tension creates an internal split: one part of us deeply wants to be seen and accepted as we are, while another part seeks to be desired and fears rejection.

So many men I've connected with online would rather not deal with explaining and defending themselves. This reluctance becomes a double closet of sorts—silence in predominantly straight communities and silence in LGBTQ+ communities.

When society only offers binary categories and celebrates conformity with them, many will choose to suppress or deny parts of themselves to avoid confrontations. That rang true for me. As an adult, I'm mostly coded as straight, and most days, it's not worth preaching or shouting about my sexuality, and I let people think what they want until it's time to correct them. Even if I'm mislabeled, I assess if the correction is worth it.

As I have gotten to know people in activist circles, social meetups, and professional collaborations, many bi+ people tend to be hypervigilant in spaces where we feel our expression of our gender can be policed—either as too feminine or too masculine to belong, resulting in a reasonable idea to avoid social situations altogether. Trust me, I get it!

PAUSE & REFLECT

If you've ever hesitated before disclosing your true sexuality or downplayed a part of yourself to fit in, what was that moment like? What did it teach you about yourself?

Over time, suppression creates disconnection—not just from others but from ourselves. Repression doesn't disappear; it resurfaces as chronic pain, panic attacks, fatigue, or other "mysterious" physical symptoms. Trauma research confirms this: when we silence our truth—our sexuality, perspective, or identity—we also mute the body's warning signals.

Have you ever known someone who seemed sick but had no clear diagnosis? This lingering weight can wear you down, aging you emotionally and physically. Some people are twenty-two but look sixty-two, bearing the toll of unprocessed pain.

This is where writing becomes a lifeline!

According to psychologist James W. Pennebaker, expressive writing for just 15–20 minutes daily over a few days can reduce stress, improve immune function, and alleviate physical symptoms. This should be paired with other modalities and explored at your own pace.

For bi+ men, this practice can be truly transformative. An article from *Psychology Today* reveals that nearly 40% of bisexual+ men struggle with mental health conditions, a rate significantly higher than their heterosexual peers. This burden often stems from external discrimination, erasure, and internalized shame. Writing provides an outlet to name and process.

Even in the chaos of life—when you can't see past the next utility bill—writing offers something within your control. By expressing your thoughts and feelings, you disrupt the cycle of repression.

Depression, anxiety, and the need to feel seen don't just sit in your mind; they seep into your cells. They might show up as shortness of breath, heart palpitations, or the compulsion to medicate through substances or risky behaviors. These struggles can feel magnified for bi+ men, who face stigma from multiple sides. But when you write, you carve out a space where your truth exists on your terms.

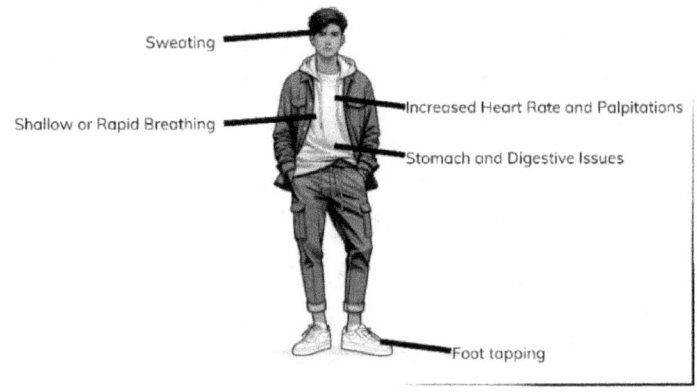

(More examples of physical sensations to be aware of)

Writing might not erase the hurt, but it can help you identify it. It allows you to take a step toward reframing your story and gradually releasing the weight that has been carried for far too long.

While ACEs provide a framework for understanding how early life experiences can shape long-term health, trauma takes many forms and affects people differently. Understanding the types of trauma—acute, chronic, and complex—helps us name and contextualize our own experiences. For bi+ men, these forms of trauma intersect with unique challenges.

TYPES OF TRAUMA

Before diving into these definitions, I want to clarify that I'm not a trauma expert or mental health professional. The insights I'll share come from my personal experiences and extensive reading on the subject, not from professional training. I also don't want your eyes to glaze over with jargon.

My goal isn't to provide clinical advice but to offer perspective and encouragement for those who, like me, need as much information as possible to reach the best version of ourselves, especially during a time when words like "trauma" are used freely and often. This section can also help you develop backstories of your fictional characters.

ACUTE TRAUMA

Think of acute trauma like falling down a flight of stairs. It results from a single, overwhelming event, such as a car accident, a natural disaster, or a sudden injury. According to *MedicineNet*, acute trauma is typically recoverable in a shorter period, three days to one month, compared to other traumas, though the emotional shock can linger.

Why is this important? Acute trauma can include personal moments of disbelief, rejection, or interpersonal violence for bisexual+ people. For example, being publicly outed by accident or on purpose, experiencing a homophobic or anti-bisexual+ slur or joke from a coworker, or facing a romantic partner's shock when you disclose can feel like emotional earthquakes. These events usually feel isolated, but their intensity can persist in the form of self-doubt, shame, or fear of future interactions.

According to the Pew Research Center, *"33% of bisexual+ adults report being "out" to most or all of the important people in their lives, compared to 77% of gay men and 71% of lesbians, demonstrating the unique stigma and invalidation bi+ people face when trying to live authentically, in contrast to other LGBTQ+ experiences."*

CHRONIC TRAUMA

Chronic trauma is like a dripping faucet in the middle of the night. You don't notice it at first, but then it's difficult to ignore. It occurs from repeated or prolonged exposure to stressful events, like abuse, domestic violence, systemic racism, or living in poverty. The National Child Traumatic Stress Network (NCTSN) highlights that chronic trauma can severely impact emotional development and often manifests as difficulties in relationships and emotional regulation, particularly in the formative years of childhood. This type of trauma is particularly relevant here because it creates a "troublesome inner child"—one whose needs were unmet and unresolved, shaping patterns that follow us into adulthood.

Why is this important? Chronic trauma includes the persistent strain of navigating a world that only offers binary scripts for sexual orientation; dating; and relationships. This might look like ongoing, continual invalidation from family members every Thanksgiving dinner, colleagues, society, TV and film, among others, which indirectly suggest you "choose a side." Such pressure might lead you to suppress your attraction in certain relationships to avoid judgment. This may also feel like repeated microaggressions, resulting in sheer exhaustion and a diminished sense of self-worth.

> *"In LGBTQ+ spaces, bisexual+ people can be seen as not queer enough, while in heterosexual spaces, our queerness makes us outsiders. This double-edged stigma leads to invisibility and isolation, creating unique mental health challenges."*
>
> — Shiri Eisner, author of *Bi: Notes for a Bisexual+ Revolution*

COMPLEX TRAUMA

Complex trauma is like a broken record that won't stop skipping—sometimes it plays smoothly, other times it scratches, rewinds, or distorts itself so badly you barely recognize the song. This involves exposure to multiple traumatic events, often interpersonal in nature, over an extended period.

We carry stories in our mind, and we carry them in our body. The heartbreak we never spoke about? It lingers in our posture. The childhood fears we buried? They resurface in the way we hesitate, retreat, or brace for rejection.

Bessel van der Kolk, a leading expert and author of *The Body Keeps the Score*, explains that complex trauma "alters the brain's stress response" and can leave individuals stuck in cycles of dissociation or numbness. For example, simultaneously experiencing abuse, loss, and a natural disaster can compound emotional wounds, making healing even more challenging.

Why is this important? For bi+ men, complex trauma can emerge from the intersection of multiple oppressions like anti-bisexual stigma, racial, emotional abuse, and physical violence, and classism and navigating a world that says your existence is inadequate, unwelcomed, and insufficient.

This includes Complex PTSD, conversion therapy, religious trauma, and invasive, coercive, or humiliating exercises. Studies show that bisexual+ individuals are more likely to report anxiety (40.4%) and depression (28.2%) than gay (25.9%, 20.8%) or heterosexual individuals (16.9%, 7.7%), largely due to discrimination and erasure (Psychology Today, 2019).

These definitions can also inspire what our fictional characters may have experienced to inform their decisions. They can also give us permission to review ways in which we may have been affected by life events.

They give form to feelings that often feel amorphous. As Bessel van der Kolk suggests, naming our experiences is the first step toward understanding and contextualizing them. It ultimately allows us to find ways to process our experiences on our own time, at our own pace, and express them if we choose.

We carry stories in our mind, *and* we carry them in our body. The heartbreak we never spoke about? It lingers in our posture. The childhood fears we buried? They resurface in the way we hesitate, retreat, or brace for rejection. Trauma is something we carry unless we find a way to release it. Now, let's explore how stories can be used as a tool for empowerment. Before we do, let's take a moment to pause and reflect.

PAUSE & REFLECT

Think of a potential character—real or fictional—who has experienced acute, chronic, or complex trauma. How does that trauma shape the way they move through their world? Do they try to bury it? Do they overcompensate? Does it define them, or do they resist letting it?

Exercise: "Roots of My Reactions"

Step 1: Think of a strong emotional reaction you've had recently (anger, anxiety, withdrawal, indifference, despair). Write it down.

Step 2: Ask yourself: *Was this reaction about the present moment, or did it remind me of something from my past?*

Example:

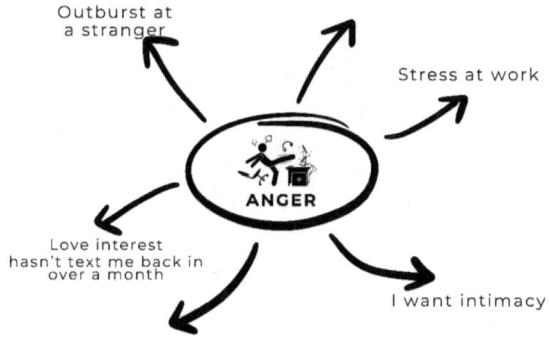

Credit: Ross Victory

Step 3: Write a letter to the part of yourself that reacted—whether it's your inner child, your anxious self, or your past self—reassuring them of what they didn't know back then.

QUICK ACTION GUIDE

CHAPTER 4 SUMMARY

- Repressed emotions don't disappear—they store in the body and can manifest as stress, anxiety, or physical illness.

- For Bi+ men, societal pressures and masculinity norms make emotional suppression even more damaging and consequential.

- Writing and self-expression are tools for release, helping to process emotions before they take a toll on mental and physical health.

3 SIGNS YOU MIGHT BE CARRYING REPRESSED EMOTIONS
PHYSICAL TENSION, EMOTIONAL NUMBNESS, RECURRING NIGHTMARES

STRATEGIES TO RELEASE STORED EMOTION
MOVE YOUR BODY: EXERCISE, DANCE, JUMP, SHAKE, JOG, WRITE, THERAPY

ANSWER NOW
WHERE IN MY BODY DO I FEEL MY EMOTIONS THE MOST? WHAT MIGHT IT BE TRYING TO TELL ME?

WANT MORE?
AT THE END OF THE BOOK, YOU'LL FIND
WRITING PROMPTS, WORKSHEETS, AND TOOLS
TO DEEPEN THIS PRACTICE.

CHAPTER 5

STORYTELLING AS A TOOL FOR EMPOWERMENT

STORYTELLING AND SELF-ADVOCACY TECHNIQUES

When we hold devalued or uncommon identities, our voices are sidelined, and our stories are told from the perspective of the dominant narrative. By telling our stories *in our own words*, we step into the nucleus of our experiences, defining our motivations, values, and outcomes on our terms. My Story. My Terms. And like so many have done before, we'll leave footprints in the sand for future generations.

> *My Story. My Terms. And like so many have done before, we'll leave footprints in the sand for future generations.*

Psychologist Robert Plutchik's *Wheel of Emotions* helps us navigate and name the emotions that shape our stories, making it easier to articulate what we feel and why. The eight core emotions are: joy, trust, fear, surprise, sadness, anticipation, anger, and disgust. Like identities, emotions are fluid and exist on a spectrum. When we understand this, we gain a fuller sense of the possibilities for expressing personal truths and the truths of our characters.

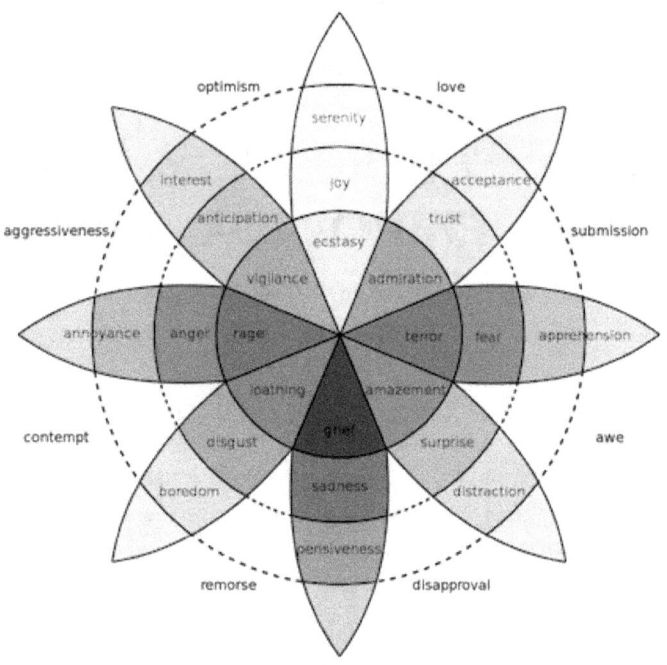

Imagine growing up in a world where every TV show and film constantly told you that you didn't exist—a world that viewed being "both/and" as if it were "neither/nor." In heterosexual spaces, you might feel too queer, while in LGBTQ+ spaces, you feel too straight.

Transforming suffering into purpose and power is all that matters. Perhaps a writer imagines a character who embraces the complexity of being "in-between" as a gift. This character might become an advocate for others, a mentor, or even a world leader. Through writing, this vision of acceptance can begin to feel real, empowering the writer to see their own story in a new light.

This act of re-authoring ripples into real life. Years of feeling invisible become proof of resilience, and sharing your testimony of strength gives others permission and courage to embrace themselves. Writing isn't a cure-all—it's raw, messy, and sometimes re-triggering. But it's also compassion, one word at a time, to acknowledge and honor our experiences.

As Ursula K. Le Guin's *The Left Hand of Darkness* illustrates, narrative can reframe how we view identity and belonging. Set on the planet Gethen, where inhabitants can change their sex by a temporary sexual cycle where they develop male or female characteristics based on their partner, the novel challenges binary norms and offers a vision of a society free from gender-specific roles. Through the eyes of Genly Ai, an envoy from another world, we see the arbitrariness of human gender roles and explore themes of identity, prejudice, and connection.

Le Guin's work reminds us that creative writing is a tool not just for self-expression but for influencing how identities can be understood. By constructing narratives that celebrate complexity and fluidity, writers can honor their truths and inspire change in the world around them.

CREATIVE EXPRESSION & BRAIN HEALTH

Imagination and fear are more connected than we might think. Picture this: you see a spider-like creature in the top corner of your wall. Its spindly legs stretch wide with detail as it clings to the wall, motionless but ready to dart at any moment. Even before your logical brain can decide if it's harmless, your body responds—your heart thuds, your breath becomes shallow, and a cold bead of sweat slides down your face.

This is your amygdala in overdrive. I hope you like science, because we're going there quickly but for good reason! Your amygdala in your brain fires red flags to prepare you to fight or flight. Muscles tense, palms clam up, and your mind races: "What if it launches toward me?" All of this happens in seconds, even if you don't know exactly what the creature is—if it's real, or perhaps friendly and cuddly.

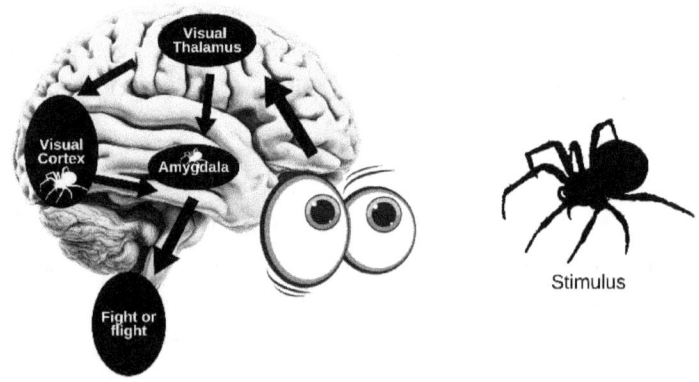

Credit: Ross Victory

Some people experience similar sensations when preparing to speak publicly. "What if I forget my words? What if they laugh? What if I fart unexpectedly?"

Your brain can still trigger the same physiological response, treating an imagined threat almost as seriously as a real one. The hippocampus joins the amygdala, encoding the experience to memory and reinforcing the association between "spider" and "danger." "Public eyes" and "danger." The result? A cycle of fear begins to grow stronger each time you imagine the threat. The expectation has been established. The tracks have been laid.

But there's good news: exposure to the stimulus can break this cycle. Whether you encounter a veiny spider in a controlled environment or imagine it in positive scenarios, repeated exposure teaches the brain that the threat isn't as catastrophic as it initially seemed. Over time, your amygdala becomes less reactive, and your body stops overreacting. Can you guess a free and effective way to expose yourself to fear? Yes, writing!

Let's say, in the context of this book, you're bisexual+ but not ready for people to know. Just anticipating pushback or imagining someone asking invasive, uninformed questions triggers anxiety, even if they never ask.

By engaging with our fear creatively, we also expose ourselves to the fears through imagined scenarios and desired outcomes, and we begin to rewire our brains. As we write more and more about our fear and engage it creatively, slowly, the imagined "danger" loses its grip, leaving us with more space to breathe and even have fun.

Keep in mind that writing and understanding how your brain works is not a magic pill, but it's a powerful (and yes, free, we love free) component to add into your self-advocacy toolbox. Some call this unlearning, while others refer to it as exposure therapy. Here, we'll call it practice and rehearsal.

Dr. Valerie van Mulukom studies cognitive networks of imagination, memory, and belief systems. Her research suggests that there's no immediate danger when the threat is imagined; repeatedly imagining it will help detach the stimulus from the expected threat since none appears. This weakens the brain's association between stimulus and expected outcome. Consequently, it also reduces the neural and physiological effects that happen in response.

"What if I'm not creative?" you may ask. "When I was a child, I collected bugs. I liked geometry and science."

Dr. Valerie suggests play, practice, and experience can foster creativity. Creativity can be *developed* and cultivated in the proper setting with examples and affirmation.

Watching fantasy films, making lists, brainstorming solutions to problems that affect your daily life, trying new foods, going outdoors, doing something spontaneous—and my favorites: experiencing foreign cultures, eating exotic foods, and witnessing new traditions—are all ways to engage the creative brain.

Neuroscientist Adam Gazzaley, M.D., Ph.D., says always having something to do diminishes creativity. Sitting still and sheer boredom can help foster creativity. At some point, you get so damn bored that you will invent something to do and pursue. Eventually, you'll start singing or cooking or something! Even going outside for a walk can stimulate new ideas.

A beauty walk is the practice of moving through the world with intention, seeking out affirmations, messages, or signs confirming your place in it. Maybe you pose a question to yourself—*Am I on the right path?*—and tune into your environment for answers. A street performer plays your favorite childhood song. A book with the exact phrase you needed appears in a shop window.

You overhear a stranger's conversation echoing a thought you just had or answering a question you've been pondering. Or maybe you experienced a similar situation like I had. One day, I opened my email and saw a promotion for Claude AI—my dad's first name—and another for JSON, a tech term that also happened to be my brother's name, Jason. A coincidence? Maybe. But the goal is to stay curious and present.

The intention of a beauty walk isn't to look for flaws. Instead, you tune into affirmations. It's allowing the world to be an ally, not an enemy, just for a moment. We spend so much time bracing for rejection that we miss the quiet ways life says, "Yes, you belong. Yes, you are seen."

PAUSE & REFLECT

If you can, take a 10–15 minute walk. As you walk, intentionally observe your environment for affirmation and permission. You can ask a question, intensely listen to a stranger's conversation, or appreciate the beauty of nature. As you walk, observe how being present makes you feel.

Imagine growing up, reaching your late twenties or early thirties and finding yourself depressed or angry for no reason.

Well, society has a way of smothering the needs, wants, desires, and joys we harbored as children. Day by day, year by year, television program by television program, post by post, we get caught in news cycles, traffic, the office, politics, and the details of others' lives.

Then, suddenly, we look around and realize that nothing around us matches who we truly are. We've become stuck in a consumer matrix where our stories don't seem to matter if we're not famous, hot, or rich according to whatever the current trend is. Corporations and billionaires end up benefiting more from our lives than we are. Meanwhile, we're on the verge of despair because of mental confinement and trying to attain an unrealistic, curated standard.

But how can we realistically acknowledge this playful child's needs to stay sane while also generating income and providing for ourselves and perhaps our family? Is the first step simply to go outdoors and ask nature questions?

Before I share some writing techniques that have helped me tap into my creativity, let's look at Jean-Michel Basquiat to drive home this inner child concept.

JEAN-MICHEL BASQUIAT

Jean-Michel Basquiat used art as an escape from his chaotic personal life. His mentally ill mother was in and out of institutions his whole young adult life. Though very intelligent, he had to drop out of school in the tenth grade and experienced homelessness throughout his life journey.

Starting off as an obscure graffiti artist, Jean used art as therapy and became an admired artist, even famous among celebrities, decades later. I believe his creative expression helped him remain alive—aat least more so than he would have been without his art—until he died at the age of twenty-seven from a heroin overdose. So, while the suffering may not disappear with art, it releases pressure off the valve.

FRIDA KAHLO

Similarly, Frida Kahlo transformed her suffering into vibrant, emotionally charged art. Born in 1907, Kahlo endured a catastrophic bus accident at the age of eighteen that left her body permanently scarred. The collision fractured her spine in several places, shattered her right leg and foot, and caused a metal handrail to pierce her pelvis and abdomen. This left her bedridden for months, enduring dozens of surgeries, and living with chronic physical pain.

Her turbulent relationship with her parents, particularly her distant and deeply religious mother, Matilde, added another layer of complexity to her life and art. Matilde disapproved of Frida's unconventional choices—her defiance of gender norms, her activism, and her marriage to the older, womanizing muralist Diego Rivera. Kahlo's mother, who adhered to strict Catholic values, also deeply struggled with her daughter's open bisexuality and refusal to conform.

Kahlo once remarked, "I paint myself because I am so often alone, and because I am the subject I know best." Her self-portraits, such as *The Broken Column* and *Self-Portrait with Thorn Necklace and Hummingbird*, depict her physical suffering, relationships, and culture. Kahlo turned her pain into beauty, making her work an enduring testament to the power of creative rebellion.

Both Basquiat and Kahlo remind us of the power of art in claiming "My Story. My Terms." Author, songwriter, watercolor artist, illustrator, baker, or cabinet maker, identity-focused art originates from our sense of self and can help release emotional valves by tapping into the energy you only have. It can save if not prolong your life!

PROMPT

Prompt: Using Robert Plutchik's Wheel of Emotions, list the core emotions that have defined 1-3 key moments in your life. How can these emotions shape a story you'd like to tell?

Expanded Prompt: Self-portrait through words. Write a short "self-portrait." Describe how your identity shows up in your emotions, body, relationships, and culture. What would you want others to understand about you from this portrait?

QUICK ACTION GUIDE

CHAPTER 5 SUMMARY

- Storytelling can help you practice resilience and rewire your brain by exposing you to your fears through written form.

- Re-authoring negative experiences can shift our perspective and allow us to create new meaning from our past.

- Emotions shape our stories and connections with readers. Using tools like Robert Plutchik's Wheel of Emotions helps us name and process emotions, making our writing more honest. Joy, anger, and fear can be turned into compelling, necessary stories.

STORYTELLING POWER MOVES

TWIST DOMINANT NARRATIVES TO MAKE THEM YOURS! INJECT YOURSELF INTO THE PLOT.

SHARE A PERSONAL TRUTH IN A JOURNAL, CONVERSATION, OR SOCIAL POST

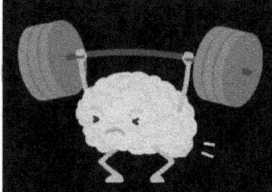

YOUR BRAIN CAN'T TELL THE DIFFERENCE BETWEEN REAL AND IMAGINED THREATS. WHEN YOU WRITE ABOUT FEAR IN A SAFE WAY, YOU WEAKEN ITS HOLD ON YOU.

WANT MORE?
AT THE END OF THE BOOK, YOU'LL FIND
WRITING PROMPTS, WORKSHEETS, AND TOOLS
TO DEEPEN THIS PRACTICE.

CHAPTER 6
INTERNAL INQUIRIES
SELF-ADVOCACY TECHNIQUES

When we ignore the whispers of our authentic selves—whether through societal pressure, fear, or avoidance—a disconnection takes root. This misalignment, existing between our internal needs and external realities, often manifests as emotional unrest and mysterious health issues we've discussed earlier.

This disconnection stems not only from the weight of societal expectations but from the unspoken agreements we've made and the internalization about who we're "supposed" to be. I've called these invisible people—the influencers, media figures, and societal commentators who preach endless requirements but are nowhere to be found for follow-up or support.

The good news? These internalized narratives and unspoken agreements are not permanent. As Benjamin Hardy writes in *Personality Isn't Permanent,* "Who you are today is not who you have to be tomorrow." Phew!

Hardy's work emphasizes that our identity, or full sense of self, is not a fixed endpoint but an evolving process shaped by the *goals* we pursue and the stories we choose to tell ourselves. This idea resonates with the journey of internal inquiry—because rewriting your story starts with asking the right questions.

IDENTIFY THE GAP

Take a moment to reflect: Are you living the story you want, or the one you were told to live? Misalignment often arises when we accept societal narratives as immutable truths. For example:

- **Societal Message:** "Real men avoid showing vulnerability and being soft."
- **Result:** You suppress your emotions, fearing judgment or rejection and end up making yourself sick.
- **Societal Message:** "Bisexuality is just a phase, or bisexual+ men don't exist."
- **Result:** You normalize downplaying your feelings, erase your identity, and try to fit into binary socially accepted categories.

Hardy's book reminds us that these limiting beliefs aren't indicative of our true selves but are shaped by external influences, paralleling the work Hardy mentioned earlier, such as family members, friends, religious communities, and social groups. The key to moving forward is identifying where these beliefs *originated* and questioning—and *choosing*—if they serve you today.

Pragmatism is key here. The journey to alignment won't always require grand gestures or public declarations. Pride parades, drag shows, and all the stereotypical LGBTQ+ cultural identifiers aren't for everyone. Identifying the gap between our actual and desired selves can be a silent, selective, meditative experience—one rooted in reflection rather than exposure and performance.

Being visible is gracious and brave but may not be suitable for your circumstances. By taking a quieter, introspective approach, you gently disrupt patterns. The gap isn't just where you feel misaligned; it's also where potential lies.

Marcus Aurelius, author of *Meditations*, once wrote, "It never ceases to amaze me: we all love ourselves more than other people, but care more about their opinion than our own." These are critical words to live by as you contemplate stepping into writing for the first time or what it means to have diverse attractions to people.

SWIM

How often do we pause to bask in the complexity of our identities, especially bisexuality?

Imagine plunging into thought, floating with these questions:

- *What gender dynamics excite you most in a relationship?*
- *What physical and nonphysical attributes do you find most intriguing?*

Internal Inquiries

- *How do you feel physically when expressing dynamics that excite you?*
- *Are there any societal expectations that influence your choices?*
- *What do you love about gender differences? What are the similarities and where do they diverge?*
- *What type of connections are possible for you?*
- *What romantic and/or sexual experiences do you fantasize about? Which experiences can you live without?*
- *What do you appreciate most about your perspective?*

PROMPT

Prompt: Think about a belief you hold about origins or your identity. Where did it come from? Does it move you closer to your goals—or keep you stuck?

Prompt: Spend five minutes in stillness. Afterward, ask yourself:

- *What does my inner voice want me to know right now?*
- Write down the first thought that comes to mind, no matter how small or unexpected it seems.

THE ROLE OF THE INNER CHILD

Reconnecting with your inner child—the version of you that existed before societal conditioning—is a powerful way to uncover your authentic desires. While the "inner child" is more of a symbolic concept, you can assign it an age based on when certain core emotional patterns were established. According to Erik Erikson's psychosocial development theory, children 0-7 years old, also known as the imprinting years, work through the stages of "Trust vs. Mistrust" and "Autonomy vs. Shame and Doubt," which shape their ability to feel secure and independent.

Jean Piaget's cognitive development theory identifies children 8-12 years old in the "Concrete Operational Stage," where they begin to develop self-esteem based on feedback from peers, teachers, and other external influences.

Hardy's concept of rewriting your story aligns beautifully with reconnecting to your younger self because it permits you to step back from the roles you've been assigned as an adult and imagine new ones rooted in your truest identity.

When was the last time you asked yourself:

- What did I love doing as a child?
- Who did I like?
- What brought me joy before life's responsibilities piled on?
- What dreams have I buried, and why?

For many of us, these questions reveal not just forgotten passions but also the fears and limiting beliefs that caused us to give up them. By listening to the voice of your younger years, you can begin to understand your deepest values and dreams, trace them—and, crucially, reclaim them.

> "Your inner child holds the key to your creativity, playfulness, and freedom—nurture them, and you nurture your soul."
> - Unknown

Internal Inquiries

Example:

In first grade, I performed "In Harmony" from *The Little Mermaid* at my school's talent show. I was nervous but thrilled, soaking in the applause as the words—"You're you, I'm me, together we can live in harmony"—rang true to me. At the time, I didn't think singing a Disney song would mark me as "different," but later I realized it had.

As I grew older, I saw how being a Black man and expressing gentleness through forms like songs, storytelling, and love notes can elicit both praise and judgment. That moment on stage, though, was pure me—unfiltered, joyful, and free. It reminds me now how important it is to honor the parts of ourselves we once shared openly without fear.

It reminds me now of the importance of honoring who we were before the world taught us to hide. Reconnecting with our inner child isn't just nostalgic and remembering the good ol' days before the world squashed our joy; it's a way to clarify your values, rebuild trust in yourself, and nurture the creativity that has always been there.

PROMPT

Prompt: Write a letter to your younger self. What encouragement would they need to hear from you today? What dreams would they remind you to pursue?

REWRITING THE NARRATIVE

Hardy's book teaches us that personality and identity are shaped by the goal setting and reaching for future and aspirational versions of ourselves.

- ☞ **Step 1: Imagine Your Desired Identity**
  Imagine yourself five years from now. What does your life look like? How do you feel about yourself?
- ☞ **Step 2: Identify the Barriers**
  What limiting beliefs or societal expectations are keeping you from living that future today?
- ☞ **Step 3: Take Small, Aligned Actions**
  Rewriting your story doesn't happen overnight. Start small—like journaling, setting a boundary, or exploring a creative outlet—and let those small actions build momentum.

PROMPT

Prompt: Describe your ideal self in one paragraph, then write down one action you can take this week to move closer to that vision. If you can't write a paragraph, think of adjectives that describe you now and adjectives that you want to describe you in the future.

What societal messages have shaped your identity? Are they still serving you, or is it time to rewrite them?

Virginia Woolf

Virginia Woolf is often remembered for her literary genius, but she also grappled with questions about identity, desire, and societal expectations. Her writings reveal a lifelong exploration of fluidity, particularly in her relationships with both men and women. In her semi-autobiographical novel *Orlando*, Woolf tells the story of a character who changes gender and lives through centuries, challenging rigid ideas of identity and attraction.

Woolf's own life reflected this complexity. Married to Leonard Woolf, she maintained a deeply loving and supportive relationship with him while simultaneously forming romantic and intellectual bonds with women, such as Vita Sackville-West. Through her writing, Woolf interrogated societal norms and allowed herself to process her layered identity in ways that resonate even today. Her story reminds us that internal inquiry isn't always about a single "answer."

Woolf's ability to weave personal truths into fictional narratives exemplifies how creative expression can be a powerful tool to reimagine, and reaffirm our identities. She used her stories to navigate her own layered identity and invite readers into a world where fluidity was celebrated. Her journey reminds us that introspection isn't about binary answers—rather, we're imagining space to exist fully, even in a world that struggles to embrace nuance.

Michael Kaiser

Michael is a 48-year-old man, married to his wife, Diane, for 20 years, and they both have two teenage kids. On the surface, his life measures up to expectations: a stable managerial corporate job, a loving family, and respect in his communities. But beneath this, Michael feels a growing sense of unease. For years, he's buried the truth that he's attracted to men, telling himself that his love for Diane is enough, that exploring his bisexuality isn't necessary or worth the potential risk of unraveling his family.

One evening, after tossing and turning for nights and an unexplained panic attack, Michael enrolls in therapy. At first, his sessions focus on stress and detachment. But as he becomes more comfortable with his therapist, he gradually begins to open up about a truth he's been carrying since he was a teenager.

When his therapist asked, "What would your younger self say about the life you're living now?" Michael felt his chest tighten. "I think he'd say he's proud, but... disappointed I never let him be fully himself." Speaking those words aloud for the first time felt like exposing a raw nerve, the truth hanging in the air, delicate but undeniable.

Internal Inquiries

This insight sparks a long process of internal inquiries, where Michael begins to reflect on how his life choices were shaped by fear, shame and doubt—fear of rejection, fear of disrupting his family, fear of being misunderstood, fear that he wasn't worthy of love.

Eventually, this leads Michael to have a challenging conversation with Diane. It's one of the hardest moments of his life. He explains the feelings he's been hiding for years and why, emphasizing his love and commitment to their relationship while also acknowledging the parts of himself he can no longer ignore.

He tells Diane that he envisions a life where all parts of him can coexist. Though the road ahead is uncertain, Michael feels he has honored himself. The byproduct of his actions will also impact his family and those witnessing his life. Some may observe this example and see scandal and deception, but I see courage and authenticity rippling outward. I see a strengthened relationship with his children and Diane and a model of resilience under pressure-cooking levels of adversity.

*

Hardy's idea that "your future self is your guide" parallels the practice of internal inquiry. By envisioning who you want to become and being guided by joy, liberation, and challenging limiting beliefs, you begin to chip away identity-based oppression and collect tools to rewrite your story in a way that feels honest and empowering.

PROMPT

Final Prompt:

- Imagine a character who embodies a part of yourself you've struggled to accept. Write a short story or journal entry about their day. What challenges do they face? How do they navigate them? How do they see themselves in the world? Who do they want to become?
- Imagine your future self is writing a letter to you today. What advice, encouragement, or wisdom would they share?
- What one step can your future self inspire you to take today?

Remember, this journey isn't about perfection. Instead, focus on the progress and being present. Every question you ask and every step you take will bring you closer. As Hardy reminds us, personality isn't permanent—and neither are the narratives that no longer serve you.

> You can run and you can hide, even if it's for decades, but whatever needs to be acknowledged will follow you a lifetime.

As you dig into these truths, please be kind to yourself. Reflection yields clarity and gems, but sometimes what you discover isn't pretty. If reconnecting with your inner child feels uncomfortable or intimidating, start small. Even a single memory or moment of joy can provide valuable insight. You can run and you can hide, even if it's for decades, but whatever needs to be acknowledged will follow you a lifetime.

CHAPTER 7

TYPES OF CREATIVE WRITING

STORYTELLING TECHNIQUES

Imagine writing a story in every genre—a memoir that reclaims your past, a poem that aches with truth, or a fantasy that bends reality to your will. Each form of writing is a new frontier, with limitless opportunities to challenge yourself. What if you didn't just stick to one lane but could experiment with them all?

Oddly, when I've told people that I'm an author, music artist, songwriter, producer, and entrepreneur, they'll feel the need to put me in a box that fits their own understanding. Even referring to myself as something general like an "artist" will elicit questions about what kind of art I create, the style of my writing, the type of genre, or which one "am I more of—an author or a music artist?" Binary thinking prevails in all areas of life.

Types of Creative Writing

When I was younger, I thought writing only looked a certain way—formal, polished, and serious. I admired the greats—Baldwin, Woolf, Shakespeare—and felt like messy journal entries or a dumb, heartfelt half-finished poem didn't belong in the same conversation. Writing, in my mind, had to be perfect to be valid. But then something happened.

In college, I used to save all my essays, stuffing them into folders like they were artifacts. One day, a guy in my class noticed and teased me: "*Why are you collecting your own writing?*" He laughed like it was ridiculous, like valuing my own words was self-indulgent.

But then I discovered Haruki Murakami, an author and musician—just like me. His narrative style was surreal yet intimate, weaving ordinary life with the strange, the magical, the unexpected. He famously wrote, "*Whatever it is you're seeking won't come in the form you're expecting.*" That line hit me hard.

> The beauty of creative writing is its variety—it's more than finding your voice. It's discovering how many voices you actually have and how they

Writing isn't about having it all figured out. It's about capturing rawness, incompleteness, all the parts that exist but are yet to be understood. The essays I saved? They weren't just school assignments. They were pieces of me.

If you've ever doubted whether your words are worth saving, what your unique mix of creative output means, or whether your crumpled-up drafts belong—they do. The beauty of creative writing is its variety—it's more than finding your voice. It's discovering how many voices you actually have and how they sound. Poetry Ross, Songwriting Ross, Rap Ross, Author Ross, and Article Ross are related but unique in the *how*. My Story. My Terms. In every format.

In this chapter, you'll unlock the doors to storytelling across styles. From catharsis, connection, or rebellion, this is your invitation to boldly go into that place. To boldly be that guy.

JOURNALING

I remember watching movies, and a character would write in a small journal after a long day, starting off with "Dear diary…" Whatever follows that remains private between them and that little book. Within those pages contain secrets, pains, and daily struggles that any person, young or old, might face.

With that being said, journaling is an effective outlet for expressing your emotions, fears, and traumas in a book that no one reads but you. It's a way of releasing your own reality without the fear of being judged. I find this type of writing helpful. In my own journaling, I try not to censor myself.

Let's be honest, sometimes we have obscene and inappropriate thoughts and desires to purge from our systems. We would never want a coworker to stumble on our journal and read about how many positions we imagined their body in or for a parent to read a passage about how much we hate them when we really love them and just need to vent. I get it. So, make sure you can protect your journals.

My dad introduced me to journaling during my teenage years. He introduced me to the idea that journals were a way to process events and document our lives for our heirs. Little did

I know that it would be his journals I discovered that allowed me to learn more about him as a man beyond his role as a father.

When I read back the words I've written, it's hard to believe I'm the same person. I also find myself grateful to be able to trace how far I've come. While there's been growth, the struggles are still apparent as well. Reflecting on past patterns helps reveal how long it took you to come to terms with certain things and celebrate how far you've come.

You'll also notice what you **don't write about** and *who* you don't write about. From my late teenage years to early twenties, I couldn't even write down that I was bisexual+ while actively knowing I was. I couldn't face the word and writing it down made it real.

Then, suddenly, I could. On the surface, that may not seem like something, but "coming out to self," was a key turning point, and journaling allowed me to archive and trace my circumstances. I now realize I was practicing resiliency by facing the fears in my words.

Once your emotions are released, they hold less power over you. I like to think of journaling as an emotional bowel movement or perhaps taking out the trash. A journal a day keeps the psychologist away! Journaling takes consistency and a nonjudgmental mindset to be effective. The ability to self-advocate is also essential, knowing that you matter and are valued no matter what feelings and thoughts you have.

Ask yourself—*am I judging what I want to write? Why?* Physically, judgment feels like hesitation or the thought, "*Should I write this? What if someone finds it?"* If you're not ready to write down what's on your mind due to fear of being judged, write about the feelings you want to express instead.

Beginner Tip: Think of a specific memory when you felt a strong sense of your identity—positive or negative. Consider any aspect of your origin, identity, or experiences. Write about what you felt in that moment and how it shaped you today..If you're unsure where to start, try writing a one-sentence summary of your day or answering the question, "What made me feel most alive today?"

Try This! Make a list of all the places you feel safe being your authentic self. If the list feels short, add places you'd like to create or seek out.

TRY THIS

Expanded Prompt: Write about a time you felt overlooked and unseen. Describe the moment and how it felt. Then, share how you would reclaim your visibility today.

PROMPT

MEMOIRS (CREATIVE NONFICTION)

A memoir is similar to a biography in that it involves writing a historical account of one's life, all told from their personal knowledge. A biography focuses more on a person's entire life, and a memoir is usually a specific period. The goal of many memoir writers is to share their stories with a wider audience while also becoming creative with their past experiences.

Celebrities often write "tell-all" memoirs to pull back the curtain on parts of their lives that have been hidden from public view, but memoirs aren't just for famous people. They're a powerful tool for anyone—a form of therapy, much like art, that helps release the pain and trauma stored within you.

My first book, *Views from the Cockpit*, began as journal entries I wrote as my father's death and familial drama began to escalate. The intention was not to write a book at first but to process all the chaos. The journals later became a creative nonfiction piece—a memoir. It uses airplane metaphors to tell the story of a father and son navigating love, loss, and hope that comes with new beginnings.

The act of writing the book and publishing it provided a deep sense of release. Reflecting on my father helped me address my inner child, and the creative process of writing and developing metaphors allowed me to shape my narrative with purpose and clarity. I'll share more about writing *Views* later.

Memoirs also give you the freedom to creatively alter situations, creating scenarios that bring emotional resolution. For example, in a creative nonfiction story, if someone who tormented you emotionally still haunts your thoughts, you can "write them off"—maybe you kill them in the story or leave them trapped on a deserted island naked and afraid, with no food or water. It may sound mildly petty (if you're like me), but it can be surprisingly satisfying.

I acknowledge that memoirs are typically seen as "factual," but writers can create a work that is part memoir/part fiction that involves altering situations to let you "kill off" someone who once tormented you.

Another memoir that brilliantly explores the complexities of identity and healing is Charles Blow's *Fire Shut Up in My Bones*. Blow delves into the struggles of growing up Black and bisexual+ in rural Louisiana, weaving together moments of deep pain, resilience, and self-discovery.

The book innovatively uses narrative structure to confront trauma, unpacking its weight and transforming it into a story of liberation. For Blow, writing wasn't just about retelling the past—it was about reclaiming it, piecing together fragments of himself, and ultimately re-authoring his identity.

Through memoir writing, whether you're grounding the narrative in strict reality or infusing it with creative liberties, you reclaim power over your story.

> *Beginner Tip: Start by jotting down 5-7 key life events that shaped who you are today. Choose one and write about it in detail.*

PROMPT

Prompt: Pick one of the events you listed. Imagine you're explaining it to someone who doesn't know you—how would you make them understand its impact on who you are today?

SONGWRITING

This is another one of my favorites! With each song, I can tell a story about a unique experience or express hope for a future outcome. No subject matter is off-limits. Telling a story in a song goes beyond speaking to my audience and also reassures me. This may sound weird, but sometimes I jam or meditate to my own music. Awkward, I know. You don't necessarily have to write pieces for others' consumption.

Just like Basquiat expressing his emotions and experiences somewhere on a building wall downtown, music is one of the best tools to soothe your soul. Adele has been known to use music to process traumatic experiences in the past. Thus, she released the pressure, found shelter in her own heart, and entertained others while making money. Aside from the entertainment value and scientifically pleasant-sounding vocals, listeners identify with Adele's music and find solace in it—almost like looking in a mirror.

Remember these lyrics, "Hello, it's me, I was wondering if after all these years you'd like to meet?" Most people in the world have used a telephone and tried to reconnect with someone or reached out unexpectedly. The point is, be true and let your truth reach who it reaches. Maybe it will be the world!

Beginner Tip: Write a two-line lyric inspired by your current mood. Don't overthink rhyme or structure—just focus on expressing yourself.

PROMPT

Prompt: Think of a moment when your fluidity made you feel powerful or conflicted. Turn that into the chorus of a song. Give your song a title!

POETRY

Poetry has a way of turning raw emotion into something transformative. It's personal yet universal, offering a way to explore identity, struggle, and triumph on our terms. Take Audre Lorde, a poet and activist whose work is foundational to identity-focused writing. In her poem A *Litany for Survival*, Lorde speaks to the precariousness of marginalized identities:

"For those of us who live at the shoreline... seeking a now that can breed futures."

These words remind us that writing allows us to carve out a space for the future we want to create, not just process where we've been. Lorde's poetry captures the tension between survival and hope, a perspective that resonates deeply for bi+ men trying to define themselves against societal norms.

In the same way, Kendrick Lamar's "Alright" feels like an anthem for resilience. He raps:

"We been hurt, been down before ... lookin' at the world like, 'Where do we go?'"

Yet, through it all, he insists, "We gon' be alright." That shift—from pain to perseverance—shows the power of reframing a narrative.

Poetry, whether traditional verse or rap, acts as a mirror and a tool for expression. It helps us distill complex emotions into words, providing clarity and release. One poet who embodies this power is Sir Nicholas Cairns, a spoken word performer and poet from Northeast England. His work explores themes of grief, love, identity, and queerness—transforming personal experiences into deeply resonant art.

With a master's in creative writing, Nicholas published *100 Small Poems* in 2021, using micro poetry to provide emotional "gut punches" and moments of realization for his readers. His work first caught my attention online when he shared pieces on grief and losing his father—experiences that profoundly resonated with me. Nicholas describes poetry as an act of authenticity: "Don't be afraid to say the bad thing..."

As a bisexual artist, he sees his identity as expansive, describing bisexual joy as "limitless," "worlds within worlds"'" and "a powerful way to be." Through his poetry, he creates space for raw, honest perspectives on grief, sexuality, and personal growth—reminding us that poetry isn't just about beauty but about truth. He also encourages poets to "embrace the cringe"—to express freely, even when it feels awkward because someone else might relate to it.

> ☞ To hear my entire conversation with Nicholas, discussing poetry, relationships with our fathers, and bisexual joy, visit the Resources page.

Whether inspired by Lorde's introspection, Lamar's resilience in moments of struggle, or Nick's gut punches, our words can reshape reality and empower ourselves and our audience.

Beginner Tip: Begin with a sensory detail (e.g., "The smell of rain" or "The taste of salt"). Expand it into a few lines about its emotional significance.

PROMPT

Prompt: Start a poem with the line, "I carry..." and explore what that means to you. Repeat "I carry" to emphasize the compounding weight.

DIG DEEPER

Dig deeper: Write a micro poem (no more than six lines) that captures the essence of grief, love, joy, or self-discovery. If you're struggling to find the rights words, start with this phrase: "I am learning that..." and let the poem unfold from there.

SPOKEN WORD

Spoken word is a form of poetry that encourages the artist to paint vivid pictures or evoke a rhythmic groove. This style often incorporates elements like call and response, refrains, and movement to enhance its impact. Spoken word is performance driven and performers typically convey their expressions to pour out their emotional jars with memorable one-liners while releasing the pain, trauma, or joy they've held onto for so long.

Sarah Kay, a celebrated spoken word artist, has become a powerful orator in this genre. Her career took off with her TED Talk featuring "If I Should Have a Daughter," where she imagines teaching her child resilience, curiosity, and how to face life's struggles with courage. Her work combines relatable stories with poetic grace, often exploring themes of identity, family, and growth. Kay reflects on handling life's challenges: *"When your boots will fill with rain, and you'll be up to your knees in disappointment... those are the very days you have all the more reason to say thank you."*

More than just a performance, Kay's spoken word serves as a bridge between the performer and the audience, offering catharsis and understanding. It's a way to use the physical body to free itself from pressure and unburden the heart.

PROMPT

Prompt: Write a short spoken word piece starting with "If I should have a daughter" (or son, child, friend). What lessons, hopes, or truths would you want them to carry through life?

NARRATIVE

Narrative writing interweaves characters, settings, and themes to create worlds. Whether fiction or creative nonfiction, narrative is limitless. This form permits every dynamic possible to explore identity, relationships, and questions that keep us awake at night.

TYPES OF FICTION

1. **Literary Fiction:**

   Stories that focus on character development and emotional depth rather than strong plot-driven actions.

   These often explore the complexities of identity and relationships.

   Example: Call Me by Your Name by André Aciman delves into desire, self-discovery, and the fleeting beauty of first love.

2. **Speculative Fiction (Fantasy, Sci-Fi):**

   These genres imagine worlds beyond our reality, offering metaphorical ways to explore themes like acceptance, difference, societal norms, and social justice.

   Example: N.K. Jemisin's The Broken Earth trilogy combines epic world-building with explorations of oppression and resilience, themes that often resonate with LGBTQIA+ readers.

3. **Young Adult (YA) Fiction:**

    YA explores coming-of-age stories focusing on identity, belonging, and the courage to be authentic.

    Example: Aaron H. Aceves's *This Is Why They Hate Us* follows Enrique, aka "Quique," a bisexual+ Mexican-American teen navigating a summer of unrequited love, personal growth, and self-discovery. Aceves uses the vibrant setting of East L.A. and the complexities of Enrique's friendships and family to ground the narrative.

4. **Contemporary Fiction:**

    Set in the present day, these stories explore the joys and challenges of modern life.

    Example: Jay Coles's *Things We Couldn't Say* tells the story of Gio, a bi Black teen reconnecting with his estranged mother while navigating a budding romance with a new boy at school. Coles skillfully intertwines Gio's personal struggles with themes of forgiveness, identity, and resilience, set against the backdrop of his close-knit church community.

HOW THEME, SETTING, AND CHARACTERS SHAPE NARRATIVE

1. **Theme:**

    Themes are the core messages or questions your story explores. In *This Is Why They Hate Us*, Aceves tackles themes of cultural identity, self-acceptance, and the bittersweet nature of love. Similarly, Coles's *Things We Couldn't Say* explores themes of familial reconciliation, self-worth, and queerness in a conservative space.

2. **Setting:**

    The setting grounds your story in a time and place, providing context for your characters' experiences. Aceves's East LA comes alive with its cultural richness, from block parties to quinceañeras, providing a vibrant backdrop for Enrique's journey. In contrast, Coles places Gio in a small-town church setting, a space layered with both comfort and constraint.

3. **Characters:**

    Characters are the heart of any narrative. Aceves's Enrique is a relatable protagonist, full of flaws and humor, whose experiences reflect the push-and-pull of self-discovery. Coles's Gio offers a poignant portrayal of what it means to rebuild trust while also finding love and identity. These characters are nuanced and multidimensional, reminding readers of the complexity of real-life experiences.

Beginner Tip:

1. **Choose Your Theme:** Pick an emotional experience or conflict.
2. **Build the World:** Create a main character and setting, which could be based on yourself or a fictionalized version of you.
3. **Confront the Conflict:** Rewrite the situation by reliving it, reimagining it, or reframing it.
4. **Resolve It:** Decide how the story ends, creating closure or reclaiming your power, or raising new questions.

Prompt: Imagine your character meeting their younger self. What advice or encouragement would they offer about this aspect of their identity?

PERSUASIVE

Persuasive writing combines logic, emotional, and ethical appeal to guide readers toward a specific action or viewpoint. It's passionate and anecdotal and can be enhanced with facts and statistics. When writing to process and heal, persuasive techniques can help you share experiences in a way that connects deeply with others and liberates your own story.

Persuasive writing may include counterarguments, challenging stereotypes, advocating for a change or policy, and encouraging or redefining concepts and labels. Persuasion encourages the reader to think, feel, or act differently by presenting a clear argument supported by evidence or emotional appeal.

Beginner Tip:

1. **Use Stories to Build Connections:**
   - Share personal stories that resonate emotionally. Instead of simply defining terms, describe the context, impactful moments, and the stakes when recognizing how it affected your life.
2. **Know Your Audience:**
   - Tailor your message to your readers' needs and values using intentional wording, examples, and context.
3. **Anticipate Objections:**
   - Acknowledge doubts or opposing views with empathy while showing how alternate views are possible.
4. **Be Clear About Your Purpose:**
   - Define your goal. What do you want your readers to think, feel, or do after reading?
5. **End With a Call to Action:**
   - Inspire readers to take the next step through reflection, writing, or advocating for a change.

PROMPT

Prompt: Write a letter to someone who has misunderstood or dismissed you, explaining why your perspective matters. Use personal stories, logical reasoning, and emotional appeals to help them see the value of your experiences and how their understanding (or misunderstanding) has impacted you.

Let's now discuss one of the most powerful and often ignored aspects of storytelling: desire. Intimacy is necessary when writing about attraction. In its purest form, it involves agency, liberation, and reclamation, especially as bi+ people. How can we write desire in a way that feels unapologetic and real?

DESIRE AND EROTIC IMAGINATION

Attraction isn't static. Bisexuals across the earth know this. It shifts, expands, contracts, and resists. Other times, it holds steady. Every bi's reason and criteria for who and why they like someone is as diverse as our identity. Some of us are more drawn to men, others to women, and some to nonbinary and trans people. We have preferences for physiques and energy—no two bisexuals are alike.

Attraction exists in the unnamable, the "can't put your finger on it" sort of lingering glance, an unexpected emotional connection and recognition beyond words. And yes, some bi+ men experience little to no sexual attraction and may identify as asexual, yet still crave intimacy, longing, and deep emotional bonds. Arousal and preferences vary because desire doesn't follow a single script. And that's where we as writers come in. Attraction can be a slow-burn indie film. Sometimes it's hentai. Or it can be a telenovela with overly dramatic facial expressions and shirtless confessions.

Whatever the formula, shame and suppression don't only disconnect us from our truth—they steal our joy. As sex researcher Dr. Justin Lehmiller says, "Sexual fantasies are one of the purest reflections of who we are." And yet, not everyone is granted the same freedom to express them. We have a lot to gain by giving ourselves permission to explore this space through written word.

Don't believe me? Straight men rap about sex with zero shame and zero consequences. Future brags, "I'm tryna f**k the DA lady in her mouth though" ("In Her Mouth"). Women dominate the charts, rightfully celebrating their sexuality. Cardi B raps in her chart-topping song "WAP," "Put this p*ssy right in yo' face, swipe your nose like a credit card."

So what's the bisexual male's equivalent? It's not like we can't flaunt our sexuality; we can and should. But...we don't. Why?

Writing about sex isn't just telling another ol' tale—it's defiance. It's inherently political. It's shattering the quiet place that straight men, gay men, and even women will never have to sit in.

Masculinity is measured by conquest, performance, and how convincingly you pretend to enjoy sports and lager. Or how convincingly you can say, "Good game, bro," while naked in a locker room. We're told who we should desire, how we should express that desire, and how often.

Society shouts and screams what "real men" do. Even the simple act of naming our attraction can feel lethal. The belief that desire—sexual or otherwise—only counts if the world recognizes it is false.

Types of Creative Writing

PAUSE & REFLECT

How can writing about shifts in attraction over time help you unpack your experiences and validate your attraction in all forms?

Through the various forms we've discussed, we can live out fantasies and erotic scenarios to reclaim moments that feel stolen. And to give language to what's felt but left unsaid. And when we name it, we liberate it.

I've felt the benefits firsthand. My poem *Unzip* plays with double meanings, what fancy folks called double entendre —on the surface, unzipping a lover's pants while also "unzipping" layers of fear and inhibition to reveal emotions.

In music, I've imagined desire boldly—by describing bodies in "Imma Look" (Latinos with tats on their backs or women with sundresses and no panties) to conjure scenarios that feel thrilling. Each time, writing turns the invisible into something tangible. Something real. And provides immense, unspeakable joy for it to exist.

Yes, sometimes it feels cringey. Writing about sex is like sending a risky text to a crush: exhilarating, nerve-wracking, and sometimes it gets stuck in draft mode, with the three little bubbles appearing and disappearing as someone contemplates their words. Articulating our likes, preferences, and desires casually, like our straight and gay family, may feel foreign at first. But here's the truth: these desires exist whether or not the world validates them and whether or not they're expressed.

PAUSE & REFLECT

How does writing about sex, intimacy, and attraction allow you to reclaim agency and joy over your own narrative?

DESIRE AS A NARRATIVE FORCE

Erotic romance stories aren't just thriving—they lead the reading market. Romance generates $1.44 billion annually, and MMF (Male-male-female) and queer erotic fiction are fast-growing categories, with authors like Katee Robert and Sierra Simone proving that readers are hungry (for more than food).

Imagine your creative take on a teenager's first kiss—one they never expected. A husband comes out to his wife after years of secrecy, both terrified and relieved when they learn to communicate better between the sheets. A man in his 70s finally allows himself to acknowledge feelings and get a girlfriend for the first time. The layers. The first nervous touch. The intoxicating thrill of being desired. Bisexual+ stories are limitless, and desire can be used as a narrative force to tell the stories we want.

But when bi+ men aren't the ones writing them, these experiences get coded and distorted by people who don't live these experiences. Bi+ male characters become plot devices—spectacles or cautionary tales. We are vampires, serial killers, homewreckers, Satan himself in the TV show *Lucifer* and characters who would (likely) be bi+ in real life but left for the audience to "decide."

Representation is intentionally curated for straight or monosexual audiences and made digestible for studio execs. But real stories? They're not about respectability—real life is about liberation.

Stereotypes are so odd. As a Black man, there are stereotypes that we excel at sports and music. That we love fried chicken and watermelon. It's true—we sometimes fit the stereotype, but not all the time. Black people can be talented dancers and singers, while others might not. Similarly, bi+ people fit certain stereotypes, and other times they don't. Some people who are bi might later come out as gay, while sometimes gay and straight people come out as bisexual. These are not flaws. This is humanity. Everyone can be anything, but who's telling the story matters.

My Story. My Terms.

Being strategic about keeping an audience engaged is an important goal, but for writers, sex, intimacy, and attraction aren't just about representation—they're about agency. Writers do a disservice to readers when we withhold experiences that can also serve to enrich readers' lives through exposure and education.

And let us not forget about humor and the possible storylines it can permit, as well as its effectiveness in reducing fear around experiences and people that seem foreign.

HOW TO WRITE DESIRE WITH INTENTION

- *Through sensory detail*—the feeling of fingertips grazing skin, the way anticipation coils in the stomach, the breath catching before a kiss.
- *Through subtext*—what's left unsaid between two people who share a glance across a crowded room.
- *Through movement*—a slow lean forward, a fleeting brush of hands, or caressing the neck.

The best stories don't state desire; they make the reader feel it. They include the audience in the scenario and circumstances, making them feel it in their loins.

PROMPT

Prompt: Write an intimate moment so vivid it makes someone blush. But here's the catch—no body parts, no explicit descriptions. Just sensation, subtext, and movement. Make it sizzle with stillness, tension, and the space between touch.

Types of Creative Writing

QUICK ACTION GUIDE

CHAPTER 7 SUMMARY

- Journaling, spoken word, poetry offer unique ways to explore identity, emotion, and storytelling.

- Each genre and style has its own superpower: journaling provides personal insight, spoken word commands an audience, and speculative fiction challenges reality.

- Creative writing is about discovering your many voices—not just one—giving you the freedom to experiment, break rules, and shape stories that reflect your truth.

HOW TO KNOW WHICH WRITING STYLE IS RIGHT FOR YOU

Do you write to process emotions and thoughts?
Yes → Try Journaling
No, I prefer performing → Try Spoken Word

Do you love capturing moments in vivid detail?
Yes → Try Poetry
No, I like creating full stories → Try Fiction

Do you enjoy exploring personal experiences in depth?
Yes → Try Memoir & Personal Essays
No, I prefer imagining new worlds
→ Try Speculative Fiction

Do you enjoy writing with rhythm and musicality?
Yes → Try Spoken Word or Lyric Writing
No, I like structured storytelling
→ Try Screenwriting or Short Stories

>>> **ANSWER NOW**
WRITE A TWO-LINE
POEM ABOUT YOUR DAY

‼️ WANT MORE?
AT THE END OF THE BOOK, YOU'LL FIND
WRITING PROMPTS, WORKSHEETS, AND TOOLS TO DEEPEN THIS PRACTICE.

CHAPTER 8
STORYTELLING FRAMEWORKS
STORYTELLING TECHNIQUES & EXAMPLES

Writers use different techniques to reveal the "heart" of every story. I'll explain a few of them here that I introduced to my students in Creative Writing class as an English teacher. These techniques have been around for thousands of years and are not solely mine or necessarily unique.

RAGS TO RICHES

I can't resist the urge to place this theme at the top because of how powerful it is among cultures across the whole world. Rags to riches stories resonate with most people, giving us a sense of hope and possibility. They tell how an individual "made it" against tough opposition. These stories can sometimes be interpreted as miracles and usually depict defying massive obstacles and odds, such as poverty, racial discrimination, misogyny, or disability, to name but a few, to achieve fame, fortune, impact, and legacy.

As you read these examples, imagine bi+ and queer men in a rags to riches story context. What story could you craft where the bi guy gets it all? Not only financially rich or rich with romantic and sexual options but emotionally wealthy after traversing a path of discrimination, including internalized and externalized stigma.

A great real-life example of a rags to riches story is from George Soros.

GEORGE SOROS

George escaped the Nazis to become one of the world's most successful investors, a billionaire, and a philanthropist. Born in Hungary in 1930, Soros survived the atrocities of World War II by assuming a false identity as a Christian to avoid Nazi persecution. After the war, he fled to London, working odd jobs as a waiter and railway porter while studying philosophy at the London School of Economics. Despite these humble beginnings, Soros built a financial empire, using his wealth to support causes ranging from democratic governance to education through his Open Society Foundations. His story exemplifies triumph over unimaginable adversity.

BRIDGET MASON

Bridget Mason was born a slave in Mississippi in the early 1800s. When her owner moved to California, she petitioned the court and won her freedom. After working for a decade as a midwife, she bought a small land plot with the money she had saved in what is known today as downtown L.A., amassing $300,000 in the late 1800s, equivalent to over ten million dollars in 2021!

Bridget, affectionately known as "Biddy," not only built her wealth but used it to serve her community, founding the first African Methodist Episcopal Church in Los Angeles. Despite being born into bondage, she became a symbol of resilience and generosity, providing shelter and aid to those in need. Her journey from a life of slavery to becoming one of the wealthiest landowners of her time is a powerful testament to determination and faith.

While these examples are one in a million and stand as outliers, the question is not how to recreate the success of Mason, or Soros, or any figure who has overcome opposition in their lives. Instead, it's about finding inspiration in their perseverance, learning the mindsets and actions that produced results, and applying those lessons to our circumstances holistically, including society's opinions about fluidity.

VOYAGE/JOURNEY AND RETURN

Some journeys don't start with a choice.

You didn't ask for this. You didn't prepare for this. And yet, here you are, fighting to survive—this is the heart of a Voyage and Return story. By the time the protagonist returns home, they are no longer the same.

HIROO ONODA

Most soldiers are in combat for months or even years, but Hiroo Onoda fought a war that had already ended. In 1944, during World War II, the Japanese military sent Onoda to the Philippine jungle with orders never to surrender under any circumstance. But when the war concluded, no one told him. He spent over 30 years hiding in the mountains of Lubang Island, believing every attempt to reach him was an enemy. For three decades, he lived in guerilla warfare, stealing food, engaging in shootouts with local villagers, and waiting for the war to end.

It wasn't until 1974—when his former commander was flown in to personally relieve him of duty—that Onoda finally returned home. But home had changed. The Japan he fought for in 1944 was no longer the same country. Onoda returned home, but did he truly come back when everyone and everything was so unrecognizable?

EUGENIA GINZBURG

Eugenia Ginzburg was a Soviet professor and journalist who was falsely accused of being a political traitor under Stalin's totalitarian communist regime. In 1937, she was arrested and sent to the extreme temperatures and brutal labor camps of Siberia, where she endured a decade of starvation, forced labor, and physical and psychological torture.

For ten years, she fought to survive the Gulags, which are forced labor camps, losing everything along the way—her home, her family, her freedom. But like a boss, Eugenia documented everything in her mind, storing every memory of suffering. When she was finally released, she returned to the world not broken but with a determination to reveal the truth in her memoir.

Journey into the Whirlwind became a powerful account of Soviet repression and personal resilience. Her Voyage and Return was more than survival—it was a testimony and warning for future generations.

Maybe your voyage wasn't a labor camp or a jungle on a Philippine island. Perhaps your journey may not have been physically grueling, but it could have been emotionally or spiritually harsher in other ways. Maybe it was heartbreak. Or a severe mental health struggle, or perhaps a toxic, dangerous relationship. You might have received a diagnosis that changed how you saw the world, endured the loss of someone you thought would always be around, experienced an unexpected accident, or dealt with betrayal. Perhaps you made the decision to "come out," only to be met with more hostility and isolation.

There's no shortage of possible "voyages." There was a before—when life made sense. Then came the storm that shattered everything we knew. And now, here you are, returning not as the person you were, but as the person you had to become.

We can call Voyage and Return survival stories where we adapt or collapse. These stories prove that we, or the characters we've developed, step into the unknown, voluntarily or involuntarily, and reemerge—bloodied and bruised but definitely stronger and wiser. At times, that's a gift. Other times, it's a burden. Either way, the journey has left its mark.

TRAGEDY

I'm not a huge fan of stories based on tragedy, though they are very effective. Marketing pain and fear is big business. Consider Non-Government Organizations (NGOs) around the world. When they air their "commercials" on TV or social media asking for donations, they put forth the most horrendous images, such as starving babies with bloated bellies, sick animals, people with missing limbs, or anything that can drive viewers to shock and tears. The aim here is to tell a tragic story and convince readers and viewers to react with a call to action, whether that means donating money, subscribing, or reposting the message.

While tragedy can be emotionally tough, it can serve as a powerful tool for education and awareness when used thoughtfully and is intended to take steps to resolve the underlying issues.

REBIRTH

Suppose you have gone through a real-life mess (divorce, sudden death, illness and recovery, estrangement, secret physical or mental abuse, significant financial hardship, addiction and recovery, or the like) and *emerged* from it. Not only did you emerge, but you also became a completely different person with new values and beliefs. You're unrecognizable in all faucets. In that scenario, you can use the rebirth technique to tell your story. Here's a fictional example:

For fifteen years, Alex was a corporate powerhouse—amassing money, power, and prestige. Every decision was calculated. People were nothing more than tools to him, and he believed rest was for losers. But at the age of 38, he collapsed on the cold floor of his glass-walled office overlooking downtown Los Angeles while an intern screamed for help.

Doctors warned him to slow down. He didn't. Drinking got worse. Panic attacks. Numbness. One day, staring at spreadsheets, it hit him—none of this mattered. So, he walked away.

Two years later, Alex resurfaced in protest camps and disaster zones. First, as an observer. Then, as a frontline volunteer, patching up wounds in war zones and political unrest. The man who once chased profit now chased ways to keep people alive.

Now? Alex runs a free medical clinic and co-founded a mutual aid program. He chooses to live modestly. He doesn't miss his old life. To those who knew him before, he is unrecognizable. His values have changed. His priorities have changed. But most strikingly? He glows with freedom. His presence is light. His laughter is easy.

Do you have a sense of your story's framework or a story you want to tell?

Are you stuck in rags, waiting for your riches?

Perhaps you've been on autopilot and never really contemplated your own story arc. Every moment you breathe, you are also writing. Maybe you know you've strayed and have lost your ability to fight to return. Don't be scared to ponder these questions and refrain from judging whatever comes up.

The fact that you're reading this book means that you know you have something you want to say; you know there are others like you who need to hear from you, but you just need some direction and a gentle push.

A story without great characters is a skeleton—structured, yet lifeless. What makes a story unforgettable isn't just where it takes us but also *who* takes us there. We don't remember *The Odyssey* only for its epic journey—we remember Odysseus outsmarting gods and monsters. We don't remember *The Matrix* just for its mind-bending special effects—we remember Neo, the nobody who became The One.

Legends aren't carved into ancient stone tablets or Hollywood scripts. Some of the most electrifying, gut-punching, and soul-searching hero stories exist in anime and comics—where characters fight, fall, and claw their way to justice. Naruto is more than a ninja; he's a kid who refuses to be erased. Spider-Man isn't just slinging webs; he's shouldering the weight of expectation while figuring out who the hell he is. Sound familiar? Let's crack open the multiverse of anime and superheroes to see what their journeys can teach us about forging our own paths.

CHAPTER 9
AN ANIME & SUPERHERO'S GUIDE TO EMBRACING YOURSELF

There are tons of bi+ folks at ComicCon. This isn't by accident. There is something inherent about anime, manga, and comics that strike a chord. And I think I'd found it out!

The most successful anime characters, like Naruto Uzumaki from *Naruto* and Izuku Midoriya from *My Hero Academia*, alongside classic superheroes like Spider-Man and Black Panther, all share a common thread: the hero's journey.

The hero's journey, similar to the voyage and return structure we've already discussed, is a classic storytelling structure. It begins with an ordinary world, disrupted by a call to adventure that often requires the hero leave behind the familiar to confront challenges that will transform them. Along the way, they face trials, encounter mentors, battle internal and external forces, and return as the person they were meant to be.

Whether navigating the streets of New York City or fighting in distant galaxies, these characters are thrust into worlds that demand conformity. Yet, they choose to rise above and carve their own paths. At the heart of these stories lies the fight for reconciliation—a quest to integrate fragmented identities, reject imposed limits, and define themselves on their own terms.

DIO BRANDO
THE BISEXUAL VILLAIN VAMPIRE
WHO DEFIES FATE

Not every character follows a traditional arc, though. Dio Brando from *JoJo's Bizarre Adventure* is not your typical anime protagonist—he's a villain who refuses to play by the rules. Driven by ambition, Dio seeks absolute power, rejecting societal constraints and embracing his status from an outcast into a god-like being who bends fate to his will. He's charismatic, ruthless, and bisexual, and his journey flips the script on what we expect from a hero. Instead of redemption, Dio pursues domination, making him a fascinating figure in discussions about agency and identity.

DEADPOOL
THE HERO WHO REFUSES TO FIT

Then there's my favorite, Deadpool, a character whose very existence mocks the rigidity to its core. Deadpool wears his complexities on his sleeve. His pansexuality isn't a footnote—it's woven into unpredictable nature like the way he flirts mid-battle sequence or jokes about his attraction to Wolverine. Deadpool reminds us that the most radical act is to embrace every part of ourselves, even when those parts aren't predictable and don't fit nicely together.

Anime and comic characters are more than sources of entertainment. They can serve as metaphors for self-definition, resilience, and breakthroughs, empowering us to say f*ck off when we're told we must fit a mold that was never made for us.

For real-life heroes like Zamo, Chongzheng, and Aaron, the battle isn't fictional—it's real life and personal. Like any great hero, their stories begin with a challenge. For Zamokuhle Zulu, that challenge started with something as fundamental as his name. As you read their examples, see if you can trace the hero's journey framework in their stories.

The Power of a Name and Self-Reunion
ZAMOKUHLE ZULU (ZAMO)

Zamo, a scholar-activist from South Africa, moves through life like Monkey D. Luffy from *One Piece*—a force of nature, unbound by anyone's expectations but his own. In *One Piece*, one of the most beloved anime and manga series of all time, Luffy is a rubber-bodied pirate with one dream: to find the legendary treasure known as the One Piece and become the

King of the Pirates. But Luffy's true power isn't just in his superhuman abilities—it's in his refusal to be anything other than himself. He doesn't conform to the world's expectations; he bends the world to fit him.

Like Luffy, Zamo isn't interested in fitting in. He builds his own belonging, drawing people into his orbit and rewriting what it means to be part of something without losing himself in the process. His strength isn't in choosing—it's in refusing. It's in integration and self-reunion.

But like any great anime journey, there will be challenges and obstacles.

A name is never just a name. It's a prophecy, a burden, an expectation. Given or chosen, a name can shape the story we're expected to follow long before we even understand it.

This is something Zamo understands deeply.

"*I have two names,*" he told me. "*Mpumelelo and Zamokuhle. And for a long time, I lived as two people.*"

Mpumelelo was the name that felt safe and predictable, fitting the heterosexual mold. But Zamokuhle? That name carried a different weight. It held the part of him that sought truth, belonging, and wholeness—a self that even he struggled to embrace for years.

"*At some point, I even hated Zamokuhle,*" he admitted. "*Because I knew the world didn't want him.*"

Zulu culture has long understood that a name is more than an identity—it's a function, a role in a larger system. Heterosexuality was once seen as duty, an obligation to expand the family lineage and ensure the continuation of the bloodline. One's worth was often tied to fulfilling that role—as a provider, a bearer of children, and an extension of history.

But what happens when your name tells one story and your heart tells another?

Anime is full of characters who fight against the expectations placed upon them. Eren Yeager from *Attack on Titan* refuses to be what the world demands—a compliant soldier and a pawn in a system built on lies. Instead, he rejects the roles imposed on him to forge his own brutal, uncompromising path.

But Zamo's battle wasn't against titans or alchemy. It was against the weight of real-life invisibility amplified by deep cultural expectations.

Moving to Cape Town—often called the queer capital of Africa—gave him the space to do what every great anime protagonist must do: integrate the aspects of himself he had been forced to separate.

"I had to remember who I was as a whole being—not just fragments of who I should be and who I can't be."

This is what naming really is. More than an identifier, it's an act of reunion and a declaration of wholeness.

Part of the work in embracing all of ourselves is understanding our name—the ones we were given, the ones we may still be searching for. And as writers, we have the power to extend that same intention to the names we give our characters.

> ☞ To hear my full conversation with Zamo, where we discuss his experience with identity, queerness in Zulu

culture, and the meaning behind his name, visit the Resources page.

PAUSE & REFLECT

Think about your own name—the one given to you at birth, the one you go by, or the one you'd prefer to have. What significance does it carry? What historical or familial expectations or assumptions come with it? If you've never thought about what your name implies or means, do you actually like your name? Do you know the story behind why it was chosen for you?

If you write stories often, what is your process in developing the names of your characters?

GEOGRAPHY OF IDENTITY
CHONGZHENG WEI

Where we grow up—the land, the culture, the expectations tied to it—shapes us before we even understand ourselves. Geography is a force that influences identity, opportunity, and even self-acceptance.

For Chongzheng Wei, a bisexual cisgender man from a small village in Southern China, geography influenced his entire relationship with queerness.

"I grew up in the mountains," he told me. "My parents were farmers. We had economic difficulties, but more than that, I had no access to LGBTQ resources, no role models. I had no blueprint for what a queer life could even look like."

His physical isolation mirrored his internal one. Without visibility, he felt alone in his own discovery. "At first, I thought I was gay," he admitted. "But then I realized— I wasn't just attracted to men. I was attracted to both men and women. And I had no idea what that meant."

Without access to representation or language, he did what many do—he turned to education in search of answers.

In many ways, Chongzheng's journey resembles Ashitaka from *Princess Mononoke*—a young prince exiled from his homeland, cursed by forces beyond his control, yet determined to carve out a future on his own terms. *Princess Mononoke* is a story of conflict between opposing worlds—nature and industry, tradition and progress, destruction and healing. But at its heart, it's about a man who refuses to choose a side. Instead, Ashitaka seeks understanding. He walks between worlds with kindness and fierce determination, believing that even in the most hostile environments, peace and truth are worth fighting for.

Chongzheng's out of the mountains wasn't just physical—it was intellectual, emotional, and deeply personal. He pursued psychology not just as a career but as a lifeline. He studied sexuality education, contributed to LGBTQ-inclusive textbooks for schools, and later, joined UNESCO in France and Thailand to work on global education initiatives. But policy work felt distant. He wanted to be on the ground.

"I realized working at the policy level was really abstract," he said. "It was off the ground, and I wasn't enjoying all the political dynamics of working at a UN organization."

So he pivoted.

He moved to the U.S., pursued a PhD in counseling and clinical psychology, and focused on bisexual mental health in China, Taiwan, and Hong Kong. His research explores minority stress and the mental health disparities faced by Bi+ people—something he had experienced firsthand.

Today, he is completing his clinical internship at Richard Donovan State Prison in San Diego, where he works with LGBTQ+ incarcerated individuals, helping them navigate gender-affirming care and build self-acceptance in an environment that is often hostile, violent, and deeply oppressive.

"Now, I help people navigate their identity in the most restrictive environment possible," he told me. "In a prison, identity is constantly under threat. And yet, even in the most oppressive places, people still find ways to be themselves."

He will soon begin his role as Assistant Professor at Santa Clara University, where he will teach, research, and train future therapists in LGBTQ+ mental health counseling.

Like Ashitaka, Chongzheng moves through different worlds—not as an outsider, but as a bridge. He has carried the weight of isolation, yet he chooses not to be hardened by it. Instead, he uses his knowledge and empathy to help others reclaim their own sense of self.

Geography isn't just about where we start—it's about where we go and how we get there.

Chongzheng's journey out proves that even when resources don't exist, people still find ways to learn, adapt, and create the spaces they once needed. He embodies what it means to do identity-focused work that doesn't only carve out a place for himself but influences the landscape for everyone who comes after him.

That's power. That's the work of a real-life hero.

When writing a character—or even reflecting on your own identity—consider:

- ✓ What expectations were placed on your character because of their birthplace?
- ✓ How does their physical environment shape their fears, desires, and self-perception?
- ✓ Do they feel a deep connection to their home or an urgent need to escape it?
- ✓ How does geography impact the work we pursue and the communities we build?

Our identity isn't just about who we are today—it's also about where we've been.

☞ To hear my full conversation with Chongzheng Wei on bisexuality, rural identity, and LGBTQ mental health in China, visit the Resources page.

PAUSE & REFLECT

How has your hometown or upbringing shaped you? Has your hometown helped you or held you back? Did your community offer visibility for someone you could be, or did you have to seek representation elsewhere? How does geography impact the way people express themselves?

EAST LOS ANGELES

AARON ACEVES & IDENTITY-FOCUSED WRITING
Creating Stories That Need to Exist

Some people survive in the world they're given. Others build a new one from scratch.

For Aaron Aceves, writing involves identity, representation, and breaking open spaces that have long excluded voices like his.

In this way, he mirrors Senku Ishigami from *Dr. Stone*—a teenage scientist who awakens in a world where civilization has been completely wiped out and vows to rebuild it from the ground up. On top of trying to survive, Senku also wants to restore art, knowledge, and progress for future generations. While he uses science as his weapon. Aaron uses words.

A bi+ Mexican-American writer, Aceves grew up in East Los Angeles, where his love for books started early. *"I fell in love with* reading in third grade," he shared. "I had to do a book report, and my mom took me to the library. I read one book, realized it was the third in a series, then had to go back and read the first two, and then reread the third one—because even back then, my mind was a little obsessive."

That early obsession with stories turned into a passion for writing books that reflected the world he knew—but didn't often see on the page.

His debut novel, *This Is Why They Hate Us*, the same book I referenced earlier in the book, is a coming-of-age story about Enrique "Quique" Luna, a bi teen navigating identity, desire, and cultural expectations in East LA. The book is sharp, funny, and deeply personal, offering a nuanced portrayal of bisexuality that challenges assumptions and subverts harmful tropes.

"Representation matters—not just in seeing yourself, but in seeing different versions of yourself," Aceves said. *"I wanted Quique to be messy, to make mistakes, to be human. We don't always get to be that."*

Like Senku reviving lost technology, Aaron creates the stories that should have always been there—ones where bisexuality isn't a side note, where Latinx characters aren't stereotypes, and where young queer people are allowed to exist in all their messy, complicated, fully human glory.

When I read *This Is Why They Hate Us*, I was transported back to my own teenage years. Quique could have been me. His struggles, humor, and attempts to give meaning to relationships and read between the lines of his classmates—it all felt so real, so familiar. And that's exactly why I reached out to Aaron to be part of *Embracing All of Me*—because stories like these give us permission to exist fully, but they also represent something tangible and more than an academic research study or a meme. They represent a life.

"I think a lot of emerging writers worry too much about what people will think," he said. *"The truth is, you can't control that. Just write the book that you need to write."*

That kind of fearless, identity-focused storytelling is what makes This Is Why They Hate Us a standout piece of bisexual+ literature. And that's the kind of storytelling that rebuilds a world, one voice at a time.

☞ To hear my full conversation with Aaron Aceves on writing bisexual characters, growing up in East L.A., and becoming an author, visit the Resources page.

Here are some key takeaways you can use on how to write identity with purpose and depth.

- ✓ Write the stories you needed when you were younger. It's that simple. If you struggled to find representations of yourself in the stories you read while growing up, write the one that should have existed. This will become your author brand and perspective.
- ✓ Use fiction to process. A different version of yourself can tell the truth better than you can in the present moment.
- ✓ Don't censor yourself for the comfort of others. Cringey is ok. Aceves' book isn't afraid to tackle sexuality, Mexican-American identity, and the realities of growing up queer in East L.A.—and that's what makes it one of a kind.

- ✓ Embrace complexity. While characters don't have to be aspirational, consider your audience and what can be weaponized in the wrong hands. Bi+ characters deserve to be, and must be, just as multidimensional as anyone else.
- ✓ Representation is about visibility and it's about liberation. The freedom to be imperfect, to take up space, and to exist beyond tragic "coming out" stories.

PAUSE & REFLECT

If you could write a story that would have helped your younger self, what would it be about? Who would the main character be? What lesson would they learn?

We know that invisibility is often framed as our greatest weakness—but what if it's actually a superpower? Bear with me!

Invisible Woman from *Fantastic Four* vanishes, but she also controls when and *how* she's seen. Her power is about shielding, strategizing, and shifting the fight on her own terms. When she makes herself visible, it matters—like when she drops her invisibility mid-battle and delivers a force field attack, turning the tide in an instant.

Maybe that's also our power. Maybe invisibility isn't just erasure—it's a strategic advantage.

We move between spaces, notice what others miss, and reshape narratives from the inside. We aren't unseen because we lack presence—we are unseen because the world ain't ready to see us.

But when we choose to be seen—like Invisible Woman—we're undeniable.

And *choosing* is power.

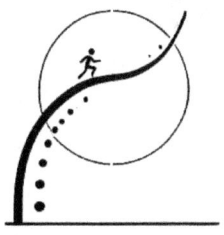

CHAPTER 10

DEVELOPING CHARACTER ARCS
STORYTELLING TECHNIQUES

What makes a character linger in our minds long after we've finished a book, watched a movie, or reflected on a memory? Is it their name or appearance? Could it be their triumphs, flaws, and contradictions that resonate with us? Perhaps it's how their journey mirrors our own.

Developing character arcs is about reflecting on journeys of change, resilience, and self-acceptance we recognize in ourselves and others. While we might forget the details about a character or a person, we'll remember how they make us feel.

Not every arc is aspirational. Some characters don't rise—they unravel. Some don't heal—they harden.

Think of Katniss Everdeen in *The Hunger Games*—a survivor who must balance resilience with her humanity. Or Harry Potter, a boy whose journey from loneliness to heroism is both magical and profoundly relatable. Then there's Tony Stark, whose brilliance and arrogance in *Iron Man* transform into vulnerability and redemption.

Finally, Celie from *The Color Purple* evolves from reticence and oppression to empowerment, highlighting her arc as a testament to inner strength and transformation.

What makes these characters so memorable? What are they anchored in? In Chapter 3, we discussed the universality of love, loss, and belonging. How do those themes translate into Katniss, Harry, Tony, and Celie?

A memorable character does more than entertain—they challenge, reflect, and inspire us.

Not every arc is aspirational. Some characters don't rise—they unravel. Some don't heal—they harden. We'll also explore arcs that challenge traditional ideas of success. Arcs that defy tidy resolutions and force us to sit with discomfort and uncertainty.

CHARACTER ARCS ACCORDING TO ARISTOTLE

In *Poetics*, Aristotle argued that character, known as ethos, and plot, also called mythos, are intertwined.

Memorable characters:

- ✓ **Act Within the Story's Framework**: They must fit the narrative's internal logic and context.
- ✓ **Have a Consistent Ethos**: Even as characters evolve and transform as the plot moves forward, their actions should reflect their fundamental essence and anchored truth. *Note: their anchored truth would likely be tied to early childhood experiences and their "inner child," as we've discussed early on.
- ✓ **Experience Hamartia**: Flaws and mistakes humanize characters, making their arcs relatable.

Aristotle also emphasized the concept of catharsis—the emotional release audiences experience when characters confront their fears or flaws, which we first discussed in Chapter 2. A character arc that includes catharsis tends to resonate the most with the viewer.

Let's consider the classic story of *The Lion King* once again. As Simba goes on the journey to take the throne of Pride Rock, he experiences (1) **LOVE** between Nala, (2) **LOSS** of his father Mufasa, and (3) **BELONGING** and reconnection to his origins in an empowered way.

Simba never ventures into a nearby city or launches into space—he evolves from a carefree cub to a courageous king in a savannah with other talking animals. The character follows a clear, immersive natural arc. Just as Simba confronts his past to step into his power, we, too, must reconnect with our inner child to champion ourselves in real life. But not everyone gets to be a king.

Not all character arcs are about glory. Some don't end in a throne or a crown. Some journeys don't lead to grandeur at all. Instead, they drag the character through the mud, forcing them to confront choices society deems irredeemable through paths few would dare to call "growth." Some evolutions aren't growth at all. Some look like hell, if not death itself.

So let me cut straight to it—can someone who's been cast aside, judged, or labeled as "too far gone" still embrace all of themselves?

TABOO CHARACTER SHIFTS

Society loves, loves, loves a good redemption story—especially when it's neatly packaged.

A prince takes his rightful place on the throne? Love it!
A ho finds God? Hallelujah!
A pastor finds pleasure? Ew.

But why?

What about the arcs we don't celebrate?

Unconventional transformations—healer to ho, student to thug—or controversial character shifts like Walt Whitman's teacher to drug lord, challenge the direction we assume evolutions should go.

I warned you this book isn't all *kumbaya* and "love and light." So let's be real for a second. I'll use a clear example of the ho phase for those who might be unaware. This is a period of time when someone may be more promiscuous than they typically are during other periods (as conjecture, of course).

- Does someone in their "ho era" deserve the same self-acceptance as someone in their "healing era?"
- Is liberation still liberation if it involves a lot of late-night texts and ambiguous decisions?
- What if the "reckless" phase isn't a detour? What if the "fuck up" is a key part of the plot?

PAUSE & REFLECT

If a character is changing, but not in the way society expects—does that still count as a transformation?

DEveloping Character Arcs

PORN TO PULPIT
THE JOSHUA BROOME ARC

Let's take a real-life example: Joshua Broome (not his porn name).

Joshua was once one of the top male porn stars in the world—rich, famous, and sleeping with model-grade women. A lot of men would call it "the dream."

But inside?

It wasn't a dream. He felt trapped, depressed, and empty. One day, a bank teller asked him if his name was really "Joshua," after recognizing him. That small interaction jolted him out of his daze. It reminded him of a self he had long forgotten. Who was he beyond his stage persona and having sex on camera?

And so, he walked away from the money and women. Now? He's a Conservative Christian pastor, husband, and father. He talks about his past without shame on podcasts and interviews and from the pulpit—not as something to erase, but as part of his story and transformation.

His Transformation in Arrows:

- Porn Star → Pastor → From adult film fame to full-time ministry.
- Emptiness → Purpose → Wealth and success didn't fulfill him, faith did.
- Shame → Redemption → He now openly shares his past without regret.
- Industry Spotlight → Spiritual Leadership → From being seen on-screen to leading in faith.
- Lost Identity → Found Calling → Once defined by his past, now driven by his mission.

We don't know all the details because we weren't there, but his story challenges common assumptions:

- Once you've gone down a certain path, you can't change course.
- Moral and ethical assumptions of someone's evolution are always incomplete.

But even with Joshua Broome's vivid example of an extreme evolution, let's ask a harder question:

Are the best character arcs those that focus on ascending to success—gettin' rich, owning the dream home, winning the heart of your crush, landing the right job, finding inner peace, or claiming the crown?

What about characters who lose everything and never rebound? What about characters who remind us how blessed we are?

MESSY ARCS

The beloved superstar can fall into obscurity. Messy arcs force us to face our own judgments about how life is "supposed to be" and how it's "supposed" to go.

Because reality says:

- Not every sex worker becomes a youth pastor.
- Not every poor kid from the projects is destined to be an entrepreneur and millionaire.

Maybe the sex worker dies from an overdose. Maybe the kid from the projects never makes it out and his circumstances push him into a world of violence. And those stories? We call them unfortunate or failure. When they're overrepresented, we call them stereotypes. But are they, really, if they represent someone's experience?

Here are character arcs we rarely talk about:

- **Loving Parent to Addict** → A person once seen as "strong" succumbs to struggle, but their fall reveals hidden pain or unresolved wounds.
- **Queer Activist to Religious Extremist** → A person who once fought for LGBTQ+ rights joins a strict faith tradition that condemns their former beliefs.

- **Therapist to Conspiracy Theorist** → A mental health professional, after years of guiding others, loses themselves in paranoia and distrust.

Not all arcs rise and overcome. Some characters look for the answer to find hell. Not everyone finds healing, and most people will never change. They're unwilling to look themselves in the face or strive for something better.

Regressive arcs matter because they mirror the truth that the weight of the past is just too much to bear. Fear can win, and self-destruction might feel better than coping.

These stories matter because they leave us with questions:

- What went wrong?
- Could they have been saved?

For every story of someone rising, there's another of someone falling. And the hardest part? We don't always know which one it will be.

Prompt: Create a character profile and write a short paragraph about a transformation seen as a downfall by society.

Consider:

- Does the character see it as a fall, or do they believe they're finally free?
- What pushed them into this new identity? Was it choice or circumstance?
- How does the world react? Are they outcast, celebrated, pitied?
- Is there another shift on the horizon, or is this where they settle?

Go Deeper:

Write it in two parts:

- First, from an outsider's perspective (a family member, a journalist, a friend who doesn't understand).
- Second, from the protagonist's perspective.
- Where do the perspectives clash? What is the "missing" piece? What is the "truth"?

LIVES IN FREEZE-FRAMES

Before she became a world-renowned poet and civil rights icon, Maya Angelou was a sex worker in her late teens—doing what she had to do to survive in a world that gave Black women few options.

Malcolm X? Before becoming a revolutionary leader, he was deep in the street life—hustling, robbing, even working as a pimp.

If history froze them in those moments, they'd be labeled "criminals" or "ho."

But labels don't tell the full story, do they? Bisexuals—we know this!

Angelou later wrote about her past without shame in *Gather Together in My Name*—owning it as part of her story, not a stain on it. Malcolm X, through prison and Islam, became one of the most uncompromising voices for Black liberation in the U.S.

A single screenshot of someone's past distorts the fight, the failures, and the fire.

Where We Focus Becomes the Truth. Do we focus on Joshua Broome's 1,000 porn films or his politics now? Do we freeze-frame Malcolm X as a hustler and pimp, or do we freeze-frame his impact on civil rights?

If we choose to ignore the full arc, the failure isn't theirs—it's ours.

Writing about complex, nonlinear character arcs challenges the binary idea that change means "success" or "failure." Just like our identities defy binaries, so do the stories we tell. Acknowledgment Is Not Endorsement. To tell a full story is not to cosign or condemn it. It is simply to tell the truth.

By writing about unconventional transformations, we reclaim the right to define our journeys without needing an approval stamp from a studio exec, a publisher, or society itself. But with this freedom comes responsibility. When a story presents an underrepresented perspective, it often becomes the only reference point for that experience—shaping how audiences perceive it as truth, intended or not.

And that? That is where our real power lies.

CHARACTERS THAT CHAMPION CHANGE THE CCC METHOD

The CCC Method provides a technical guide to crafting layered characters who resonate deeply with readers. It uncovers the emotional, psychological, and social dimensions of a character's journey, ensuring that their growth feels authentic, complex, and reflective of real-life complexities.

Memorable characters like Celie, Katniss, Tony Stark, and Harry Potter, along with memorable public figures like Nelson Mandela and Frida Kahlo, and modern celebrities like Beyonce, wrestle with tension between their *wants* and *needs*, which drives perceptions of their choices and creates conflicts but also champions change.

- *Wants* are external and surface-level: "I want to be seen, loved, or accepted."
- *Needs* are deeper: "I need to accept myself first before I expect others to."

A character might *want* notoriety and public success to escape their family's expectations, only to realize they *need* to confront their upbringing and redefine what success means on their own terms at their own pace.

Imagine what fears, doubts, or contradictions your character carries. How do their identity markers, such as gender, race, and experiences, intersect to create biases and tension? What changes must they champion to overcome those limitations? Use the checklist below to help you contextualize your character.

1. **Change**: Is the character evolving? Always answer yes to this!
2. **Conflict**: What challenges—internal or external tensions—fuel their shift?
3. **Champion**: By the end of the story, does the character become an advocate for their truth or values, inspiring other characters in the story (or readers) to reflect on their own journey or take action?

QUESTIONS TO ASK ABOUT YOUR CHARACTER TO CRAFT OR UNCOVER THEIR CONFLICTS

- **Identity**: What identity markers matter most to them? Which do they downplay or "cover"?
- **Fear**: What keeps them awake at night?
- **Blind Spots**: What critical weaknesses are they unaware of?
- **Secrets**: What do they conceal from others?
- **Embarrassment**: What situations make them feel vulnerable or exposed?
- **Motivation**: What drives their actions, and what risks will they take to achieve their goals?

I'll provide a poignant example.

Let's say you have a bisexual+ character named Bobby. He grew up in a hyper-masculine environment with an emotionless father figure who emphasized his participation in activities like sports and hunting.

Bobby's character arc could begin with him rejecting his same-sex attractions to "fit in," motivated by his attempt to gain his father's approval, only to discover that suppressing his attractions leads to disconnection from family, friends and romantic partners, fearing their rejection and disapproval. He may even lash out at those he suspects to be similar to him, conforming strongly to expectations of how men should be and who men should like.

Bobby's arc could chart the messy process of embracing all of himself—the seen and unseen aspects, the internal conversations, the unrequited love, and the constant tug of war between their public self and private desire. These are universal human themes. At the end of his arc, Bobby becomes a champion for himself and for others, propelling the audience to ask questions, take some type of action, or gain a new awareness to apply in their lives.

Again, conversations around the tension between our wants and needs aren't unique to bisexual+ men. But when you write with an identity-focused lens, you can directly explore cultural dynamics that often remain below the surface—dynamics around geographic location, class, income, race, gender, and how these factors impact the conflicts and the solutions we seek.

Here are some pop culture examples!

In TV: Walter White (*Breaking Bad*)

- **Change:** Walter evolves from a mild-mannered chemistry teacher to a powerful and morally corrupt drug lord.
- **Conflict:** His desire for respect and acknowledgment and his external fight against rivals drive his transformation.
- **Champion:** Though his journey is dark, Walter's arc forces viewers to <u>confront questions</u> about ambition, power, and morality.

In Books: Offred (*The Handmaid's Tale* by Margaret Atwood)

- **Change:** Offred begins as a woman resigned to oppression under Gilead's regime but gradually finds her voice and agency.
- **Conflict:** Her internal resistance grows as she risks everything to rebel against the regime's brutality.
- **Champion:** Her journey <u>sparks conversations</u> about autonomy, power, and resistance, making her a figure of quiet defiance.

In Film: Chiron (*Moonlight*)

- **Change:** Chiron evolves from a shy, bullied boy to a guarded but self-possessed man.
- **Conflict:** He struggles with his sexuality, identity, and the traumas of his upbringing.
- **Champion:** By reconnecting with his past and embracing his vulnerability, Chiron <u>becomes a symbol</u> of resilience and self-acceptance.

In Real Life: John Amaechi, who redefined masculinity and identity in sports

- **Change:** As the first openly gay NBA player, John Amaechi transformed how masculinity and sexuality are viewed in professional sports, challenging stereotypes about LGBTQ+ athletes.
- **Conflict:** Amaechi faced expectations about hypermasculinity and homophobia within the world of basketball, balancing his public identity with private struggles.
- **Champion:** Post-retirement, Amaechi became a psychologist, author, and advocate for diversity, equity, and inclusion, inspiring LGBTQ+ youth to embrace their identity and break through ceilings.

In Real Life: Amanda Gorman, from speech impediment to National Youth Poet Laureate

- **Change:** Amanda Gorman, the youngest inaugural poet in U.S. history, overcame a speech impediment to become an articulate and powerful advocate for justice and equality.
- **Conflict:** Her journey required perseverance in the face of self-doubt, systemic inequalities, and the pressure of performing on the global stage.
- **Champion:** Through her poetry, Gorman advocates for social change, blending themes of hope, resilience, and activism. Her work, like *The Hill We Climb*, has inspired a generation to believe in their potential.

 Prompt: Think of a real-life figure who embodies the CCC Method. How did they:

1. Embrace transformation?
2. Overcome conflict or societal expectations?
3. Use their platform or journey to inspire others?

Write a short scene or monologue from their perspective, focusing on a key moment of growth into a champion.

SHOW, DON'T TELL

The adage "show, don't tell" urges writers to use descriptions and dialogue, allowing readers to experience the story rather than be told what's happening.

- **Example of Telling**: Denise was angry at her father.
- **Example of Showing**: Denise slammed her smartphone onto the damp kitchen counter, her hands trembling. "Why does he always talk to me like I'm stupid?"

Showing invites readers into the scene using specificity (words like slammed, trembling, counter, etc.), allowing them to interpret emotions and motivations themselves with their senses.

How?

- Select action verbs that are observable (slammed, trembling, etc.)
- Select vivid adjectives that evoke the five senses and describe various traits and qualities (damp, etc.). Avoid using "very" and replace it with a stronger adjective. For example, "a very neat room" can be "an immaculate room."

DEVELOPING A CHARACTER BRAINSTORMING ACTIVITIES

- ☞ **Collaging**: Gather visual inspiration (photos, fashion, settings) to conceptualize your character's appearance or environment.
- ☞ **Journal Entries**: Write a journal entry in your character's voice, focusing on a pivotal moment in their past.
- ☞ **Naming**: Choose a name that reflects the character's cultural background, personality, or story theme.
- ☞ **Backstory**: Develop a brief history that explains your character's current motivations and struggles.
- ☞ **Desires and Motivations**: Define what your character wants—and why it matters.
- ☞ **Relationships**: Sketch connections between your character and others in the story. How do these relationships push them to grow or hold them back?
- ☞ **Character Arc**: Outline how your character transforms over the course of the story. What lessons do they learn?

EMBRACING ALL OF ME

AVOIDING TROPES, STEREOTYPES & BIAS

When crafting characters, we aim to create "people" and layered, compelling, and authentic portrayals. However, stepping into identities or experiences outside of our own requires care. Misrepresentation can alienate your audience and perpetuate biases with real-world consequences. This can happen, even if we share communities.

- ☞ A bisexual+ writer can still reinforce confusion and cheater tropes.
- ☞ A feminist writer can still flatten female characters into "strong" but never vulnerable.
- ☞ A Black writer can still unintentionally center colonial perspectives.

Because bias isn't about who is telling the story—it's about what the story focuses on and which elements are placed in the "freeze frame."

TRY THIS

Try this! Write about a moment where you felt misrepresented. How would you tell it differently today?

Misrepresentation is a freeze-frame of a full reel. When we misrepresent, we tell an incomplete story—we trap characters in a single moment, reducing them to their lowest point, their struggle, their trauma.

Like we discussed:

- Malcolm X the hustler vs. Malcolm X the leader.
- Maya Angelou the sex worker vs. Maya Angelou the poet.
- A ho in their hoe phase vs. the full complexity of why, how, and where they're going.

The Challenge: Push Past the Freeze-Frame. Where we focus becomes the truth we tell. As writers and consumers of stories, our challenge is to push past the freeze-frame.

Our job is not to make characters "likable" or "redeemable." Our responsibility is to make them whole—to write what's true. To understand the power of freeze-frames and to push past them—to serve the story and serve the audience.

In identity-focused writing, we give permission to ourselves and our readers to be flawed, evolving, and contradictory.

And that? That's the reason we're here.

When writing outside of your lived experience, ask:

- Does this character perpetuate harmful stereotypes about a/my group? Is this my intention?
- Are they one-dimensional, defined solely by an identity instead of their humanity? How can I add conflict? Where can I add more depth and complexity?

- Is my character or portrayal grounded in cultural or personal specificity?
- I can't make everyone happy, but have I sought input or perspectives from those who live this experience to minimize any potential harm?

Take, for example, *Sex and the City* and its portrayal of a bisexual+ man, Sean. When Carrie Bradshaw learns about Sean's bisexuality, she reacts with skepticism, dismissing it as "a stop on the way to Gaytown." Her dialogue and the attitudes of her friends reinforce harmful misconceptions about bisexuality, framing it as a phase and mockery.

Although Sean is portrayed as charming and confident in his sexuality, his bisexuality is reduced to a quirk—something incompatible with Carrie. Rather than validating bisexuality as legitimate and enduring, or just allowing the audience to make up their own mind, the show uses Sean's identity as a plot device to emphasize Carrie's perspective and doubles down with their critique, further marginalizing bisexual+ men in real life and fueling myths about our credibility.

At its peak, *Sex and the City* reached ten million viewers per episode and extended its cultural grip through books, movies, and spin-offs. A show beloved by urban, educated women in their 20s–40s, it wielded immense influence over perceptions of relationships, gender, and female sexuality.

No, it isn't solely to blame for the struggles bi+ men face. But when a show this big reinforces harmful stereotypes—when it mocks bisexuality and flattens identity into a plot device that people can remember decades later—it doesn't just reflect culture. It creates it.

This is a show set in New York City, one of the most diverse places in the world with over 8 million residents (home of the immigrant processing capital of Ellis Island), yet somehow there's a lack of sexual fluidity, and we often only see a few Black, Hispanic, or Asian people appear in the background, usually as trash truck operators or gang members.

Six to ten million people tuned in. MILLIONS laughed along. They walked away thinking they'd learned something substantive about love, sex, and relationships. And when the credits rolled, these messages didn't just stay on-screen—they seeped into boardrooms and bedrooms. They shaped dating norms and self-perceptions. They whispered to millions of real-life Carrie Bradshaws—and their closeted boyfriends—that a relationship with a bisexual+ man isn't a thing.

Be gay. Stay closeted. Or die.

And if this show was the blueprint, then what does that say about the house culture has built? Who's in it? Who's locked out?

The question isn't if media like this has harmed us. That answer is obvious.

The question is: What will we do to flip the script?

PROMPT

Prompt: Write a short scene where one of your characters realizes what they want (e.g., recognition, love) isn't what they truly need (e.g., self-acceptance, forgiveness). What internal or external events lead to this shift or "aha" moment?

Prompt: Rewrite a new scene for Sex and the City. Instead of Carrie dismissing Sean's identity, explore how she could approach the conversation with curiosity and respect.

Consider:

- How could Sean share his experience in a way that reflects confidence?
- How might Carrie react if she asked thoughtful questions? What could their dialogue look like if it validated bisexuality as legitimate and multidimensional?
- How would her interactions with her friends be influenced if Carrie remained interested in Sean?

Expanded Prompt: Add a moment where Carrie reflects on her own biases after being corrected by Sean. How might this change her understanding of herself?

CHAPTER 11
Writing as Rebellion Writing for Liberation
SELF-ADVOCACY TECHNIQUES

"Your intuition knows what to write, so get out of the way."

- Ray Bradbury, Author

In *1984*, George Orwell introduced Newspeak, a language designed to control thought by controlling words. By removing the language for rebellion and deeming it a "thoughtcrime," the government made resistance impossible.

People suspected of thoughtcrime were taken by the Thought Police in the middle of the night—arrested, tortured, or randomly disappeared.

Many who committed thoughtcrime became "unpersons." Unpersons had no records. No memories. No photos proving they had ever lived.

Even when the government, Big Brother, rewrote history and records were destroyed, the term "unperson" ensured that no one had the language, context, or mental framework to question or even conceive of resistance. Eventually, people stopped fighting because they feared the Thought Police and lacked the language.

Winston, the last man who remembered the time before Newspeak, was tortured until he surrendered. In the end, his obedience became devotion.

And that's the risk we face if we don't rebel and refuse to be erased—a world where bi+ men no longer push back against the narratives handed to us. This is not even a word where we accept scraps or crumps, this is a world where we stop existing.

A world where we stop naming ourselves, seeing ourselves, and believing we ever existed. The question is—will we let it happen to us?

Newspeak Term	Real-World/Cultural Parallel
Unperson	Bisexual men erased from history as "gay" or "straight"
Thoughtcrime	Banning LGBTQ+ discussions in schools
Doublespeak	Politicians using "family values" to justify anti-queer policies

Erasure is more than a dystopian concept. It's more than bisexuality.

In 2022, Florida passed the Stop WOKE Act (HB 7), restricting discussions of systemic racism and banning critical race theory in schools and workplaces. This erases historical context, making it easier to ignore past oppression and deny the impact of discrimination today.

On January 20, 2025, The Trump Administration kicked off President Donald Trump's second term by signing an executive order "Defending Women from Gender Ideology Extremism and Restoring Biological Truth to the Federal Government," which states that it is the policy of the United States to recognize two sexes, male and female, requiring all federal agencies to adjust their policies. This is most obvious because of the Trump Administration's revocation of the Obama administration's decision to *allow* openly trans people to serve in the military.

When a government, fictional or real, strips words from language, history, and policy, it rewrites reality—erasing us from records, ultimately daring us to forget we were ever here.

THE POWER OF CREATIVE REBELLION

Artistic rebellion reshapes wills imposed upon us by society. Jean-Michel Basquiat, through his chaotic, brilliant works, challenged the elitism within the art world and highlighted social injustices. In works like "Hollywood Africans" and "Irony of a Negro Policeman," Basquiat's bold, electric colors and fragmented, defiant words shouted their truth, which I interpret to be: **You will not overlook me or my perspective, and you cannot reduce the intricate, vibrant complexity of my existence.**

Creative rebellion becomes a sledgehammer to shatter oppressive scripts, carving out bold spaces where nuance is acknowledged and celebrated.

In fiction, Jeffrey Eugenides' *Middlesex* unravels the multi-generational saga of Calliope "Cal" Stephanides, an intersex individual grappling with identity, belonging, and self-discovery. Using Cal's narrative to dismantle rigid binaries, the novel delves into intersections of gender, sexuality, and heritage across continents and decades.

Through rich, visceral language, Eugenides challenges readers to see identity as fluid and multifaceted, offering a mirror to those navigating spaces that defy societal norms. This story underscores the power of embracing complexity and rejecting labels—a hallmark of identity-focused writing.

Similarly, Octavia Butler's *Kindred* reimagines the historical narrative of slavery through the lens of Dana, a Black woman from the 1970s who is inexplicably transported to the antebellum South. As she confronts the brutal realities of her ancestors' lives, Dana's journey forces readers to grapple with the legacies of trauma, resilience, and survival.

Butler's work is a masterclass in blending speculative fiction with raw emotional truth, illustrating how narrative can focus on connecting past and present while mirroring back the emotional weight of systemic oppression.

Even the horror genre offers profound opportunities for rebellion, as seen in *Candyman*. This film transforms a gruesome urban legend into a critique of systemic racism, gentrification, and the cyclical nature of violence. *Candyman* forces audiences to confront the uncomfortable truths of collective trauma. More about the horror genre and its link to identity-focused writing later.

Music also has the power to confront societal norms and resonate for those of us navigating fluid identities. Music offers a visceral, immediacy to channel rebellion into melodies, beats, chants, whispers, and cries. Artists across genres have used their craft to break, remold, dismantle, and create spaces where complexity of genre and identity is celebrated.

Take M.I.A.'s "Paper Planes." The catchy beat hides harsh truths about how immigrants and refugees are treated. With gunshots and cash registers woven into the track, M.I.A. flips the script on harmful stereotypes, forcing listeners to confront the realities of systemic oppression. Her music doesn't seek permission to exist—it demands recognition, making her an emblem of creative defiance.

Janelle Monáe's "Dirty Computer" is another striking act of rebellion. Through her exploration of queerness, Black identity, and gender fluidity, Monáe dismantles the rigid norms that have tried to box her in. Tracks like "Pynk" celebrate the beauty of individuality and freedom, while the album's narrative arc reimagines a world where difference is not just accepted but revered. Monáe's work reminds us that creativity is a declaration of self-worth.

For Frank Ocean, rebellion takes on a soothing, introspective tone. His album *Blonde* rejects genre conventions and delves deeply into personal themes of love, loss, and bisexuality. Tracks like "Self Control" and "Nikes" offer a tender, unflinching look at the complexity of attraction and identity.

For many Black bisexual+ men, Ocean's refusal to conform to expectations—musical or societal—have paved the way for navigating spaces of fluidity and sparking cultural conversations.

Björk's *Homogenic* is a sonic rebellion that redefines what it means to create personal, avant-garde music. Blending Icelandic folk influences with electronic beats, the album channels themes of individuality and cultural identity. Tracks like "Hunter" reflect Björk's journey of self-discovery, shaped by the pressure to constantly evolve. "I thought I could organize freedom," she sings, exposing the tension between control and surrender, between personal agency and the expectations placed upon her.

These works and creators illustrate that rebellion can be subtle or it can be aggressive and provoke. Creative ceilings are self-imposed. Writing that explores identity, such as the bold works of artists like Jean-Michel Basquiat and M.I.A., the time-bending trauma depicted in *Kindred*, or the stark and violent realities presented in *Candyman*, transforms the writing process into a confrontation with oppressive forces.

Rebellion can be exhilarating but also intimidating. Imposter syndromes often lurk, whispering that you aren't enough or your story isn't valid or unique enough. It will convince you that silence is safer and that you should be grateful where you are. It sounds like having a common story means it's too common to stand out. You may wonder: *"Am I a real writer if I haven't published anything?"* or *"Does my story even matter if others don't understand it?"*

The answer lies in the act of writing itself. Writing about fluidity, your layers, and identity will feel daunting, especially since there are so many uncontrollable ways people will interpret your words. Especially if you don't fit the image they expect. Writing gives you back what the world tries to take. My Story. My Terms. It doesn't have to be polished for it to be powerful. Rebellion isn't always loud and brash. Sometimes rebellion is quiet and personal.

In college, my sexuality consumed my thoughts, layered with the pressures of classes, midterms, and the looming transition into adulthood. I was trying to name it, see it, and control it—afraid that if I didn't, it would take over my life.

> Writing gives you back what the world tries to take.

I had been calling myself bisexual+ since I was 16 or 17, but I had no roadmap for how to exist in it calmly, especially since I had little dating or romantic experience with any gender. A bisexual's love life can be compared to a slow-loading video: buffering, stalling, and never quite getting to the good part. I just wanted to get to the good parts! Everything people assume bisexual+ men are doing at 17? Oh yes, I would've loved that!

The world around me didn't reflect my feelings in a meaningful way. I feared that part of me wasn't real or lasting—especially in a transitory time like college—and that, like a magician's trick, the "truth" would eventually reveal itself as something else. What I didn't realize was that my sense of self was enduring. I just couldn't force the world to mirror it back to me.

Many men I've connected with over the years—men who discovered their bisexuality between puberty and later teenage years—have shared this experience with me. The uncertainty, the over-analysis, the intrusive "What if?" questions.

For some, this manifests as what I discovered was called Sexual Obsessive Compulsive Disorder or Sexual OCD—a cycle of forbidden thoughts, compulsive questioning, and an almost paralyzing fear of one's sexuality, sometimes even self-disgust. **Have you ever experienced this?**

Clinical psychologist Dr. Steven Phillipson describes Sexual OCD as an obsessive, fear-driven questioning of one's sexual orientation—not a reflection of actual desire or identity. Unlike natural self-discovery, SO-OCD turns uncertainty into an exhausting mental loop, a relentless need to "prove" one's sexuality rather than simply experience it.

I was once in a men's group discussing anxiety and religion when one man said something that caught me off guard. He had once prayed to God for two things:

1. To reveal his true sexuality.
2. To make him either fully gay or fully straight.

I had never heard those words spoken aloud before. Until that moment, I thought I was the only one who had cast that prayer.

How unfortunate that instead of experiencing queerness as exploration—as many of our straight counterparts do during adolescence—for some of us, it becomes an obsession, a dark voice, an equation to solve rather than an experience to live.

And when it comes to these obsessive thoughts—about our orientation, what it means, and the endless imagined scenarios—speaking them aloud can feel impossible and unfathomable. But while we may not always know how the OCD develops, we do know this:

Like that veiny spider we discussed earlier, lurking in the corner of the wall, our job is not to fear the thought of it but to recognize that it holds no real power over us. Spiders, our sexuality, others' eyes, our origins, all of it. We have been conditioned to react a certain way. But intrusive and obsessive thoughts specifically lose their grip when we engage with them intentionally by getting out of our heads with:

A pen.
A beauty walk.
A competent therapist.
An effective prescription.

We don't have to stay trapped. We gotta get out of our heads!

It might take a jolt—like losing a father or someone or something you believe is permanent in your life—to shake you into awareness. And like a strong ocean tide rolling in, everything shifted when I lost him. Grief stripped away my dad, my best friend—but also my fears. If I had already lost so much, what was left to lose by trying something radical like vulnerability or authenticity? I decided to test all those theories from the social media gurus and thought leaders about vulnerability, manifestation, and "being the change." I wanted to see if vulnerability actually paid off.

That's why identity-focused writing is a radical act. It's not about fitting into a dominant narrative—it's about stating your truth. It's also about listening and being attuned to those inner pushes.

But the first step is giving yourself permission.

Permission to ask:

- ? **What do I actually like?**
- ? **What gives me endless joy?**
- ? **What truly represents me?**
- ? **What is real for me, even if it's confusing, all over the place, and doesn't fit what others expect?**

Grief forced me to ask those questions. Writing *Views from the Cockpit* permitted me to answer them. In answering them, I gave myself permission to take on more risks—risks that not only led me to deeper truths about myself but also pushed me to confront social and professional risks to seek more opportunities to connect with readers, speak at conferences, and uncover a whole new version of me where my professional, personal, and creative interests could intersect and coexist. And yet, even with all this growth, I sometimes still wonder—did I wait too long?

PAUSE & REFLECT

Have you ever held back from expressing a truth about yourself because you weren't ready? What stopped you then, and what might need to change for you to express it now?

Writing your truths, creating speculative worlds, blending genres, or penning a memoir becomes an act of defiance, both for the writer and for those portraying underrepresented experiences. Writing as an act of rebellion isn't limited to attacking society and penning scathing critiques (alone)—rebellion is also about liberation and generosity. It's creating a space where all of you is seen and there*bi* becoming a lighthouse to others on a similar path, and those who may just be witnessing your life.

"You write in order to change the world, knowing perfectly well that you probably can't. But also knowing that literature is indispensable to the world... The world changes according to the way people see it, and if you alter, even by a millimeter, the way people look at reality, then you can change it."

– James Baldwin, Author and Activist

PRACTICING THE ART OF NOT GIVING A F*CK

Embracing a "not giving a f*ck" mindset isn't a casual decision. It's exhilarating and terrifying. And when I say, "Don't give a f*ck," I essentially mean being more devoted to your craft and more committed to your personal development than focusing on the judgment of others. Judgment and opinions will not go away, but you can prioritize yourself to reduce the effects of judgment.

In the summer of 2023, I decided to drop a song called "Bisexual+ Daze." The song opens with a man at a club, his mind filled with thoughts that he's never had like being approached by a hot couple at the bar, asking himself if these thoughts are real or a result of the secondhand weed smoke. It's a story of fantasy and joy, but it's more than that—it's about letting my sexuality breathe through my art, free of shame or restraint.

Writing these types of songs can feel thrilling and nerve-wracking because, let's face it, hip-hop isn't overflowing with lyrics about bisexual male experiences. Even in a genre known for pushing boundaries, I sometimes wondered: *Am I doing too much?* On top of the fact that rapping was never something I aimed to do.

I sometimes find myself second-guessing. *Is this too explicit? Will it isolate me? Am I narrowing my career by sticking with this direction?* I've even watered down lyrics at times, trying to aim for what I think might appeal more broadly.

But at the end of the day, there's a balance to strike. Living in this bubble where I see bi+ experiences as central, it's easy to forget that my audience isn't all bi or bi men. So, "not giving a f***" really comes down to honoring whatever creative instinct I'm feeling at the moment—trusting that my story has value, even if it's not universal.

This isn't something you master overnight. You don't wake up with fully grown courage; you build it step by step. For me, each project has been like testing the waters. When I dropped "Bisexual+ Daze," it was the first time I'd put something so bold and overt into the world. And sure enough, the response was mixed. Some people loved it, especially those within my community, while others reacted with Bible verses or the usual chorus of "bisexual+ men don't exist."

But that experience taught me something valuable: my role as a creator is simply to create, be authentic, and share. How people choose to process or handle what I put out isn't on me. What's more, I discovered that I'm resilient enough to do it again and again. So, practicing "not giving a f***" is really about taking that first step, seeing what happens, and building the strength to keep going.

> "The purpose of a storyteller is not to tell you how to think, but to give you questions to think upon."

– Brandon Sanderson, Fantasy and Science Fiction Writer

On *The Pivot Podcast,* President Barack Obama shared a deep truth many overlook: when you sit in rooms with powerful people—CEOs, celebrities, even royalty—you realize they aren't all that. He cautions the audience that their titles and bank accounts don't make them any more deserving than you. Don't let anyone make you feel like you don't belong. They're not as smart, special, and sophisticated as you believe. And that's coming from someone who has met kings, queens, and world leaders.

Keep that in mind as we move into the next section about self-doubt.

1. Overcoming Self-Doubt in Writing

"What if I'm not a good writer?" is a common fear. Imposter syndrome will rear its head as you begin writing.

- Authentic expression is the goal, not technical perfection.
- Focus on capturing the emotion behind the story, not every detail.

- Start with short pieces or fragments—don't pressure yourself to write a "perfect" story.
- Write for yourself first; worry about sharing later.

2. Stop trying to please everyone

You can't be happy, nor can you fully take care of yourself, while trying to make everyone else happy. I once visited Sequoia National Park and was amazed by the skyscraper-sized trees. Have you ever noticed how these trees grow and mind their business? There are hundreds of other trees of various sizes and ages, and the tree focuses on its purpose by growing and bearing fruit with zero concern about what the next tree is doing.

Trees also do not compete. They are literally centered in *their* being and *their* purpose. To be clear, your healing is your responsibility. Other people's healing, including your mom, grandma, and brother, is their responsibility. I know life is complicated, and we are tied to people emotionally, financially, and in other ways, but how much are you willing to invest in yourself?

3. Find people who speak your language

A rotisseur and a baker are both cooks, but the baker probably isn't the best person for the rotisseur to consult on a safe temperature to serve meat. You will have to get out there and look for people who will understand where you've been and, more significantly, where you want to go.

In California, we have a restaurant chain called El Pollo Loco, known for its Mexican-style grilled chicken. They serve up rice, beans, tortillas, and burritos. How wise is it to roll up to an El Pollo Loco drive-thru asking for a greasy burger and fries? Read the room. Find people who speak your language.

Writing is protest. Writing is freedom. We can also name our fears, give them form, and—better yet—defeat them outright through the horror genre. Horror isn't just about the boogieman in the closet. It's about survival.

Let's discuss monsters!

CHAPTER 12

HORROR AS A LENS
STORYTELLING TECHNIQUES

Boogeyman in the closet. Shadows that brisk by when no one is looking. A high-pitched screeching in the dark. A chainsaw revving in the distance.

Horror has never just been about monsters—it's about fear, survival, and power. Horror is the epitome of identity-focused writing because it forces us to confront what defines us.

- Horror is about who gets to belong.
- Horror is about who gets to be feared.
- Horror is about who makes it and who doesn't.

Isn't this the underpinning conversation we've been having this whole time? When we strip stories down to their essence, all that's left is: **Bias. Hierarchy. History.**

Every horror story has a monster and a villain. In the best horror, monsters and villains are stand-ins for real-life terror:

racism, misogyny, homophobia, anti-bisexuality, transphobia, islamophobia, antisemitism, loneliness, illness, poverty, all the things! Horror, especially through an identity-focused context, permits us to externalize oppression to personify the evil that plagues our lives. To acknowledge it, name it, face it to break it!

Let's quickly zoom in on phobias.

Phobias are about what we can't control. Tight spaces (claustrophobia), spiders (arachnophobia), darkness (nyctophobia), snakes, heights, and more. But phobias also pertain to the fear of difference. This is where we get words like homophobia, transphobia, islamophobia, xenophobia.

People who embody those words like to resist and debate their use of them because they don't think of themselves as "afraid." But fear, like everything else, is complex. Fear isn't always the jump-scare kind—it's aversion, dismissal, hostility. In horror, phobias manifest as monsters. In life, they manifest as bias, laws, and cultural exclusion. Different language. Same fear.

Fear isn't always the jump-scare kind—it's aversion, dismissal, hostility. In horror, phobias manifest as monsters. In life, they manifest as bias, laws, and cultural exclusion. Different language. Same fear.

*

What if the villain isn't a sadistic masked slasher—but a system that punishes those who don't conform?

What if the real terror isn't Leatherface but technology that provides anonymity while users commit violent acts through faceless profiles? Imagine an online forum where strangers orchestrate real-world attacks, or a livestream where an anonymous audience eggs on a crime in progress—cruelty at the click of a button.

What if the monster isn't Jason Voorhees but corporate policies that are put in place to remove lifesaving services to increase shareholder value?

And what if the real monsters aren't evil dolls like Annabelle, Megan, or Chuckie but a mass media that spins and sensationalizes global events for ad revenue? Take, for example, the early days of the COVID-19 pandemic. TV networks didn't cover it as purely a public health crisis, but as a ratings war, amplifying fear with dramatic death toll counters and images of dead bodies piling up at New York's Central Park, as we watched helplessly from our living rooms. In a world where fear drives profits, the most frightening thing isn't a haunted doll—it's the industries cashing in on our anxiety.

The villain is never just a villain, are they? Villains and monsters are a summation of parts, and to think of them otherwise would be to oversimplify and become the same bias that plagues us as bisexual+ men.

But let's take that even further.

In an earlier chapter, I talked about identity like layers of a cake—layers of experience, history, and contradictions. Yes, the same is true for villains.

Hannibal Lecter wasn't only a refined cannibal—he was a survivor of wartime trauma. Erik Killmonger (*Black Panther*) wasn't only a ruthless antagonist—he's shaped by constant systemic injustice.

Even Dracula, in some versions, is more than a bloodthirsty monster—he's the lingering ghost of historical fears, conquest, and loss. Let's even say your boss or ex, and while they may be a villain to you, they're more than just your boss or ex. Often these villains view themselves as heroes or saviors in their own narrative.

> *Terrifying monsters are also revealed in mirrors.*

When we write villains, we have to ask:

- ? What made them this way?
- ? Are we seeing them at their worst moment, or is there more to know?
- ? Would they be the villain in a different context?

Terrifying monsters are also revealed in mirrors. What if we're someone else's horror story? What harm have we justified based on our experience and identity?

As writers, truly compelling villains don't just haunt the protagonist—they force us to confront parts of ourselves we'd rather keep buried.

For bi+ men, horror is training. The most compelling horror isn't about the monster—it's about those who learn to outmaneuver it. Horror lets us sharpen those instincts and ask: Do we slip through the cracks, rewrite the rules, or burn the whole system down? In horror, survival is more than just making it to the end—it's about deciding what kind of world is worth fighting for.

Before we break down how to fight monsters, let's quickly examine how horror stories have always reflected societal fears.

WHO'S THE REAL VILLAIN?

Every culture has legends of terror. The most enduring legends aren't about fanged creatures and troubled spirits—they reflect struggles, injustices, and unspoken truths of the societies that create them. To start, we'll review some case studies from London.

FRANKENSTEIN (1818)

I'd be remiss not to incorporate one of the most well-known horror stories of all time. Mary Shelley's *Frankenstein*. The real horror of *Frankenstein* isn't the creature created in the lab—it's what the world does to him.

- He wasn't evil.
- He wasn't violent.
- He just wanted to exist.

And the world looked at him and said, "Hell No!"

Sound familiar?

"Othering" turns people into monsters. And the real question is, who is the monster? The world or the creature that others them? The time period and social environment also contribute to the stories we tell.

Frankenstein was written during a time of rapid scientific advancements and industrialization. Looking back, the book reflects societal fears about the consequences of unchecked technological progress and the loss of humanity in an increasingly mechanized world.

The novel was initially published anonymously on New Year's Day in 1818. Mary Shelley was only 18 years old when she began writing her horror novel—and 20 years old when the first edition of *Frankenstein; or, The Modern Prometheus* came out.

GEORGE ROMERO'S NIGHT OF THE LIVING DEAD (1968)

Released during the Civil Rights Movement, *Night of the Living Dead* redefined horror by using the zombie apocalypse as an allegory for racial tension.

What made it revolutionary? Ben, the film's protagonist, played by Duane Jones, was a Black man in a leading role—something unheard of at the time. Unlike the stereotypical portrayals of Black characters in 1960s cinema, Ben was intelligent, strategic, and resourceful, taking charge of a group of white survivors.

But the film's real horror isn't the undead—it's the zombie-filled world he's trying to survive in. After making it through the night, Ben is shot by a white mob mistaking him for a threat, his death eerily mirroring the racial violence and systemic injustice of America.

Romero didn't just make a horror film—he made a statement: when society breaks down, its deepest prejudices rise to the top. And the biggest threat among zombies is still a Black man.

CHRISTINE (1983)

Stephen King's *Christine* is about a possessed car with a mind of its own, stalking and killing those who threaten its owner. If you haven't seen this classic, this is a must-watch. Christine isn't just a pretty, polished car—she is unchecked hatred, an obsession that grows more violent the longer it goes unchecked. Christine, like prejudice, doesn't need a logical reason to wreak havoc. She harbors jealousy and is territorial, running over anything in her way. Growing stronger over time.

ONRYŌ

In Japan, Onryō spirits are vengeful ghosts, often women who have suffered betrayal or violence. They return not solely to haunt but to demand a reckoning. These women aren't born evil; they were wronged first, and their wrath develops from being silenced and denied justice. Onryō spirit stories remind us that pain doesn't fade—it lingers and will eventually demand a response.

DJINN

In many Middle Eastern and South Asian horror traditions, Djinn represented spirits but were also stand-ins, metaphors for forbidden desires (especially those deemed "taboo" in society like forbidden love, gender nonconformity, queerness, and personal ambition that goes against tradition), societal transgressions, and the unseen forces that shape us.

Like Candyman's generational trauma, Christine's unchecked fury, or Frankenstein's creature being shunned before he even speaks, these stories show us that monsters are made, not born.

What happens when identities are denied?

When a system forces people into silence?

When wounds are left to fester?

Horror answers these questions with unsettling clarity:

What we ignore doesn't disappear. It lingers. It festers. And when the moment is right, it comes back with a vengeance.

PAUSE & REFLECT

- *What is your favorite horror story and why?*
- *What fears have shaped your life?*
- *If your fears were a monster, what would they look like?*
- *How would they move, sound, or act?*
- *What societal monster impacts bi+ men the most?*

DISMANTLING THE MONSTER
STRATEGY > STRENGTH

Once we name the monster, we have to figure out how to defeat it. The fight is the point. Here are a few techniques protagonists use to defeat the monster. On the Plot Structure, this would be a falling action on the way to the conclusion. Pay attention to which strategy resonates for you in preparation for your exercise to create your own monster.

1. Discovery of Weakness

Every monster has an Achilles' heel. Maybe it thrives on ignorance. Maybe it crumbles in the face of truth. What is the monster's greatest fear?

(*Example:* In A Nightmare on Elm Street (1984), *Krueger loses power when people stop fearing him and "face him." What happens when we stop fearing those who try to control us and stand up to them?*)

2. Weaponizing the Monster's Power

Some protagonists survive by taking what makes the monster powerful and flipping it. We can expose absurdity by using the fear and ignorance that fuel discrimination. This is one of my favorites. Humor, radical visibility, and over-exaggeration can often strip the monster of its power.

(*Example:* In Dracula (1897), *Van Helsing and his team use Dracula's own weaknesses, like garlic and holy water, against him.*)

3. Outsmarting the Monster

Survival is about thinking ahead and strategy. If the monster relies on fear, what happens when we refuse to be afraid?

(*Example:* In Get Out (2017), *Chris doesn't escape through brute force but by understanding how his racist captors operate and using their own tools against them.*)

4. Making Alliances

No one survives a horror movie alone. Who are your allies? Who can amplify your voice?

(*Example:* In It (2017), *Pennywise thrives on isolating kids. But once they come together, his power weakens, unable to face the collective force.*)

5. Move in Silence

Not every battle is fought loud and proud. Defeat can mean knowing when to act and knowing when to wait and be quiet.

(*Example:* In *The Invisible Man (2020), Cecilia outsmarts her abuser by waiting for the perfect moment to expose him.*)

6. The Upper Hand

What happens with the tables turn? What happens when the protagonists have a strategic advantage they didn't realize at the time? And the protagonist gains more power, access, strength, or knowledge than the monster? What happens when the hunted becomes the hunter?

(*Example:* In Halloween (2018), *Laurie Strode is no longer just a victim—she activates and prepares for Michael's return and fights back.*)

There are more:

Escape (Choosing a Different Path)

- Some horror stories don't end with the villain's defeat. The hero sometimes escapes the cycle instead of fighting it. The real victory may be choosing not to play by the monster's rules.

Showdown (The Final Battle)

- Audiences love a good showdown. In the climax of a horror story, the protagonist stands their ground against all odds. They are willing to die and sacrifice for it. The cost is high, but the gain is higher.

Safe (For Now...)

- Perfect for trilogies and series. Horror stories may not end with everything wrapped up neatly in a bow, but the hero will carry scars and be forced to move forward differently if not avoid the monster and put distance between them.

Which of these strategies speaks to you? What kind of fighter are you?

Oppression can feel like a never-ending battle between David and a supersized Goliath. But every monster has a weakness. Every system has a crack. The question isn't just "What are we up against?" but "What do we have within our control?"

We can fight monsters by playing their game or rewriting the rules entirely. But make sure the story ends with us winning.

R.L. Stine, author of the famous *Goosebumps* books, said, "When I write, I try to think back to what I was afraid of or what was scary to me, and try to put those feelings into books."

TERRORS TO EXPLORE IN THE HORROR REALM

Darkness and shadows
Isolation
Jump scares
Supernatural entities and abilities (ghosts, demons, defies physics, etc.)
Gore and body horror
Psychological manipulation
Confined spaces
Unpredictable/unstable antagonists
Creepy dolls and toys
Distorted or disfigured faces
Curses or forbidden objects
Haunted locations (abandoned buildings, graveyards)
Mysterious, surveillance, cryptic messages
Insects or swarms
Possession or mind control
The unknown or unexplained phenomena
Desperation and survival
Doppelgängers or impostors
Apocalyptic or end-of-world scenarios
Phobias

PAUSE & REFLECT

Imagine a character coming face to face with a monster that represents a real fear or bias. How does the monster try to manipulate them? Use one of the terrors above to explore creatively.

Think of a time when you faced a metaphorical "monster" in real life. Did you fight, escape, or outsmart it? How did it change you?

CHAPTER 13
DEVELOPING YOUR WRITING PROCESS
STORYTELLING TECHNIQUES

Now that we've explored how identity shapes our emotions, let's turn our attention to the technical aspects of structuring a story. Stories require heart and form. We'll focus on the craft of writing—building characters, structuring stories, and refining your voice.

Writing tends to be a solo sport, requiring you to sit for hours with a singular focus on words and sentences. The level of persistence, and frankly, boredom cannot be underscored, but this journey doesn't necessarily have to be done alone.

Having a community around me has been essential—a group of people who share my identity and perspective but also who genuinely understand what it's like to create long-form pieces, and folks who let me know that what I'm creating matters. Being surrounded by folks who "get it" and who value your perspective makes it easier to keep pushing, even if your music, your lyrics, your stories don't receive the engagement you anticipate.

Your creations won't be for everyone and not being for everyone is what makes it *necessary*. Let's imagine that you have surveyed the archives of your life to become the authority of your perspective. You've decided who and what matters. What happens next? Next is developing a process around your strengths and getting organized around some technical components of writing.

> *Your creations won't be for everyone and not being for everyone is what makes it necessary.*

The writing process for a memoir, a speculative fiction short story, a persuasive piece, or a novel has a structured approach consisting of key phases: brainstorming, outlining, drafting, editing, rewriting, and finally, polishing the finished product.

Organizing your thoughts with the goal of publication can be challenging, so I will draw on Aristotle's historical perspective to provide you with fundamental insights.

While Aristotle's framework provides a strong foundation for creative writing genres like fiction, memoir, and poetry, journaling and freewriting stand apart. Journaling and free writing prioritize raw expression and personal reflection instead of structured plotlines.

Journaling and freewriting can also be used as "source material" for structured pieces. This type of freewriting captures the emotional core, which you can keep for yourself or later shape into a narrative using Aristotle's structure.

But now, since we have a strong foundation of the benefits of identity-focused writing, we'll discuss using beginner-level strategies on how to form the writing into a cohesive narrative.

BUILDING BLOCKS OF A STORY

With the courage to explore your story set, let's examine the building blocks that can help you shape your narrative into something cohesive and impactful. Aristotle wrote *Poetics* around 335 BCE, making it one of the oldest surviving texts on writing.

Though ancient, his ideas are more relevant than ever—they are the framework for many modern storytelling. From Hollywood blockbusters to intimate memoirs, Aristotle's observations continue to influence how stories are told and understood today.

At its heart, *Poetics* emphasizes that every great story has a structure—a beginning, middle, and end. Think of this as your own "coming-out journey," which probably also had a beginning (realization), a middle (struggle), and an end (acceptance/ questions).

Aristotle introduced the concept of "dramatic unity," meaning that stories should have a clear focus and progression. Clear focus and progression are particularly important for identity-focused writing, where our goal is not only to share emotionally rich experiences but also to create a sense of purpose. Below is an example of a basic plot structure.

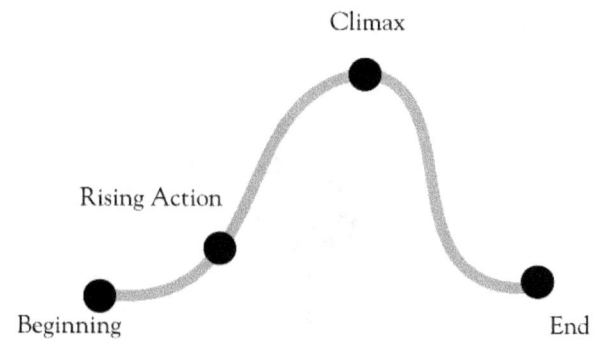

Credit: Ross Victory

While Aristotle's framework was originally designed for plays and epic poems, its principles translate to all writers.

Consider this simplified three-act structure based on his teachings:

- **Act 1 – The Setup:** *What conflict, questions, and characters sets your story in motion?* For identity-focused writing, this could be an early experience of misalignment or self-doubt.
- **Act 2 – The Confrontation:** *How does the character (you or a fictionalized character) face this challenge? What choices are made, and what obstacles result?*
- **Act 3 – The Resolution:** *What growth or insight emerges from this experience?* Identity-focused writing should leave the door open for further exploration and a call to action. The end should reflect a shift in understanding and perspective. An easy way to think

of this is a character championing a change. What change do they want? What action should the audience be inspired to take?

Here are three key takeaways from *Poetics* you should know as a writer:

1. **Plot Is King (But Not the Only King)**

   Aristotle called plot (*mythos*) the "soul of a story." It's the chain link of events that moves your character from conflict to resolution—or, in identity-focused writing, from a question to a deeper understanding. Even when the focus is on personal growth, there needs to be a sense of cause and effect, an unfoldment that keeps the reader invested.

   Ask yourself: What foundational question drives my story? How does each event or moment push it forward? How are the external and internal forces evolving?

2. **Characters Drive the Plot, Not the Other Way Around**

   Aristotle emphasized that characters (*ethos*) need to be consistent and relatable, even in their flaws. This means that your identity, values, and struggles should shine through in every decision your "character" makes.

In memoirs, fiction, or poetry, your audience should feel your humanity using universal emotions of love, loss, and belonging. Tip: By the end of your story, the internal and external worlds of the character should have evolved.

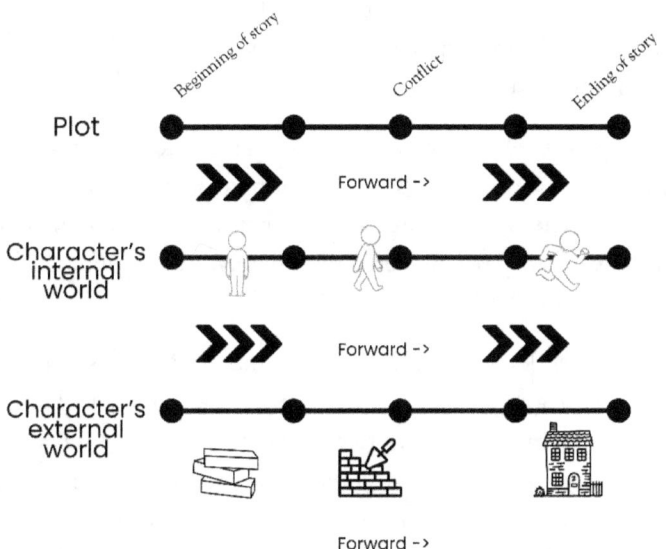

Credit: Ross Victory

3. Catharsis

One of Aristotle's most profound contributions is the idea of *catharsis*—a term we touched on earlier. In identity-focused writing, catharsis often comes from the vulnerability of sharing struggles, triumphs, and lessons. It allows readers to see themselves in your words.

When I began writing my horror story *Egg* during the COVID-19 pandemic, it began from an idea I couldn't let go—a boy named Nakoa Jamar who, after a mosquito bite on his 12th birthday, begins to develop an evil Siamese twin in the center of his chest. Even though the concept was strong, I had no idea how to structure it in a way that would keep readers hooked.

Far too often, stories ease into their premise instead of gripping readers immediately. But readers don't owe us their attention— we must earn it!

I thought back to a creative writing class I took in college. My professor warned me of a common mistake for new writers: delaying the hook. Far too often, stories ease into their premise instead of gripping readers immediately. But readers don't owe us their attention—we must earn it!

So I started *Egg* with a sense of unease—Nakoa's birth. The delivery room is sterile and quiet—too quiet—until a nurse begins acting strangely, her movements unsettling and her presence *off*. There's a palpable sense that she's aware of something that everyone is oblivious to. I wanted readers to sense that something was *wrong* from the very beginning.

Egg isn't just about body horror—it's about emotional horror. As Nakoa grows older, his twin isn't just a physical representation of suffering, it's also the voice in his consciousness, a forced manipulation of his choices that he cannot escape. By structuring the story around milestone birthdays—12, 18, etc.—I was able to pace out his slow unraveling, letting the tension build over time.

When the truth is finally revealed, it forces the reader to rethink everything they've read. The body horror was just the surface. The real terror was who Nakoa was becoming—the reasons behind it, and how he and his family would have to "adapt or collapse" to the new circumstances.

I didn't have the structure of *Egg* figured out when I started writing. I didn't know my chapters would be based on birthdays. I didn't know that "eggs" would also be symbols for new beginnings. The act of writing revealed the shape of the story, which was refined over time.

Whether it's horror, memoir, or something in between, structure is what keeps readers turning the page—holding their breath—ready for the next reveal.

HOW TO ORGANIZE YOUR STORY

1. Beginning, Middle, and End

    If this is your first time organizing a story, simplify your plot into an easy-to-follow three-act structure.

    Note: Even if you're writing memoirs or personal essays, the three-act structure exists to help you organize your narrative and is not a a rule.

    For example, you can think of the three-act structure as a way to develop your story by understanding your sexuality. The beginning represents the realization, middle signifies the struggle and pushback, and the end marks the acceptance, or lingering questions.

- **Beginning (The Setup):** Introduce your characters (yourself or fictionalized versions), setting, and the central question or challenge.
- **Middle (The Conflict):** Show the struggles or growth. Include emotional or external challenges that unravel and propel the story forward.
- **End (The Resolution):** Reflect on what's changed—what did the character learn? Who are they now? What action should the audience take?

2. Climax (The Turning Point)

Define the climax as the emotional high point or moment of change in a story.

- **Make it relatable:** This is the 'aha' moment where something shifts—when the main character (you or a fictionalized version) realizes something, confronts someone, or makes a decision that changes everything.

3. Exploring Endings

Identity-focused narratives are never truly finished. Unlike traditional narratives that end with resolution, identity-focused stories mirror life itself—messy, ongoing, and full of unanswered questions. These aren't stories that close; they are stories that evolve and call readers to action.

Note: Before you start writing a story, consider the takeaway, the main lesson, or the ending so that you'll have a clear direction for your narrative. Plots, much like our lives, move forward.

Review the plot structure of The Lion King for a popular basic example.

Plot Point	Beginning	Middle	End
	Describe your main characters and the world they live in	*List the major events and obstacles your hero faces. What are the stakes?*	*Describe the final, most intense conflict or challenge.*
Introduction of Characters, Setting, & Themes	Simba, Mufasa, Scar; Pride Rock, African savannah	-	-
Initial Conflict	Scar plots to overthrow Mufasa and get rid of his son Simba	-	-
Rising Action	-	Mufasa's death, Simba's exile from the Pride lands	-
Turning Point	-	Nala finds Simba and convinces him to return to Pride Rock as King.	-
Climax	-	-	Simba battles Scar to reclaim Pride Rock
Resolution	-	-	Simba becomes king, restoring order

Also review the plot structure of my story Egg for a basic example from a fellow writer.

Plot Point	Beginning	Middle	End
Introduction of Characters, Setting, & Themes	Ron, Shanise, Nakoa, Marcus, Danica	-	-
Initial Conflict	On his 12th birthday, Nakoa finds a mosquito bite that turns into a Siamese twin, Marcus.	-	-
Rising Action	-	Nakoa and Marcus age, their bond worsens; Marcus's wild behavior isolates their family.	-
Turning Point	-	Marcus drugs Nakoa to control their combined body, eventually killing their dog and destabilizing their family.	-
Climax	-	-	Nakoa attempts to drown Marcus in a bathtub, unable to

			coexist any longer.
Resolution			The twins separate as Marcus retracts, leaving the family to find new normalcy.

PROMPT

Prompt: Think of a time when you reached a turning point—where you couldn't go on living the same way. What led to that moment? How did you feel before, during, and after?

Expanded Prompt: Organize a fictional story using short sentences like the examples of The Lion King and Egg above.

- What sets the stage (the beginning)?
- What obstacles or realizations occur (the middle)?
- Where is the character now with their circumstances? (the end—or the next beginning)?

CHAPTER 14

STRENGTH VS. WEAKNESS WRITING ASSESSMENT

STORYTELLING TECHNIQUES

"We all have a story. The difference is: do you use the story to empower yourself? Or do you use your story to keep yourself a victim? The question itself empowers you to change your life."

– Sunny Dawn Johnston, Psychic

It's not easy for a first-time writer to spot their own weaknesses. My first book took two years to complete because I scrambled around like I was lost in the dark at every stage. I hadn't yet completed the full cycle of book writing, so I struggled to trust the process. Spotting your strengths is important because it helps you focus on areas where you excel and identify specific elements to address as you improve your weaknesses.

Once you develop the mindset to write with confidence, it's time to create your writing reasons. Writing reasons fundamentally address the question: why are you investing so much time in *this* project and *this* story?

Essentially, what is your intention and motivation for writing? Below is a table-style self-assessment that will help you rank yourself in key areas on a scale from 1 to 5. Fill in the chart while thinking about your writing reasons.

WRITER'S SELF-ASSESSMENT
RATE YOUR SKILLS

Use this section to check your overall understanding and action items. For each skill area, select the box that best represents your current level, from 1 (Needs Work) to 5 (Excellent).

Exploring Identity Themes

☐ I feel unsure (or fearful) about incorporating identity into my writing.

☐ I include identity themes but struggle to give them depth.

☐ My writing touches on identity but could be more specific or impactful.

☐ I write about identity in ways that are meaningful and relatable.

☐ My work explores identity deeply, offering new insights and universal connections.

Vulnerability & Connection

- ☐ I find it hard to write openly about my experiences, even to myself.
- ☐ I can write about personal topics but often hold back and fear rocking the boat.
- ☐ I share personal stories but could be more vulnerable or authentic.
- ☐ I write with honesty and openness, creating emotional connections with readers.
- ☐ My writing is raw and deeply vulnerable. I don't center others in my writing.

Plot and Storytelling Structure

- ☐ My stories feel aimless or lack clear direction.
- ☐ I struggle with pacing or creating a compelling middle.
- ☐ My plots are functional but could be more dynamic or engaging.
- ☐ I craft cohesive plots with strong arcs and satisfying resolutions.
- ☐ My plots are masterfully structured, keeping readers invested from start to finish.

Building Characters (fiction & memoir)

- ☐ My characters feel flat or lack distinct personalities.
- ☐ I have some character development but struggle with depth or growth arcs.
- ☐ My characters are interesting but need stronger motivations or flaws.
- ☐ I create layered, multidimensional characters that readers connect with.

- ☐ My characters are vivid and memorable, driving the story with their actions and choices.

Technical Skills: Grammar & Fluency

- ☐ My grasp of grammar and punctuation needs significant improvement.
- ☐ I understand the basics but often make errors that require correction.
- ☐ My technical skills are solid, though I occasionally need to brush up on rules.
- ☐ I write with technical accuracy and confidence, needing minimal revisions.
- ☐ My technical proficiency elevates my writing, enhancing clarity and style.

Technical Skills: Sentence Structure

- ☐ My sentence structures are repetitive or lack variety.
- ☐ I experiment with structure but often fall into predictable patterns.
- ☐ My writing includes varied sentence structures, but some need polishing.
- ☐ I use sentence structure effectively to enhance the tone and pacing of my work.
- ☐ My sentences are dynamic, artfully crafted, and flow seamlessly.

Motivation & Discipline

- ☐ I struggle to make nonnegotiable time for writing and stay consistent.
- ☐ I start projects but often lose momentum.

☐ I write consistently but need better time management or goal-setting.
☐ I stay motivated and work steadily toward my goals.
☐ I am highly disciplined and achieve writing milestones with determination.

☞ To download a PDF copy of this checklist, visit the Resources page.

PROMPT

Prompt: What did you learn about your writing strengths and weaknesses from this checklist? What's one small action you can take this week to level up in one area?

1. What are your strongest skills?
   - Reflect on the areas where you checked 4 or 5. How can you use these strengths to enhance your style and voice?
2. What areas need growth?
   - For categories rated 1 or 2, brainstorm one step you can take to improve (e.g., reading more dialogue-rich books, attending a workshop, etc. These will become your action items).
3. Track Your Progress:
   - Revisit this checklist as you grow in your writing journey!
4. Print out the "Daily Habits Checklist" to establish a routine

GOAL SETTING AND EXPECTATIONS

As a writer, setting straightforward goals that are easy to understand can be difficult. Your writing reasons and expectations after writing must align harmoniously. You can't afford to pursue a goal that completely contradicts what you hope to achieve. If your expectation is to reconnect with yourself, then set goals along the lines of writing that resonates with you. If your goal is to build a skill to brand yourself as a writer or craft a top-selling series, take the time to study trends that are working and not working in the book market.

Below are more questions you can ask yourself to help identify your intentions.

- Do you want a completed manuscript to shop for an agent?
- Do you want a completed book for legacy purposes?
- Do you want to fulfill the goal of publishing a book?
- Do you want your book to be sold in stores, online, or both?
- Do you want a high-profile review of your work (e.g., *The New York Times*)?
- Do you want to be famous?
- Do you see your book becoming a TV series or film?
- How much time are you realistically willing to spend to accomplish your goals?
- How much money are you willing to allocate to the production of the book? First-time writers might not know the total costs involved, so you may overshoot this or undershoot like I did.
- Do you want to sell the book or offer it for free (or both)?

TIPS FOR TIME MANAGEMENT AND DISCIPLINE

"Eat bitter, taste sweet."
— Chinese Proverb

Let's be real: finishing what you start is hard... Like, really hard. Writing takes time, energy, and willpower—and life will throw every excuse in your way to make you quit. The nature of this work isn't exactly sexy and luxurious, and if you're like me, it's often done in the dark and in random places.

Have you ever met someone who's been working on the same film script for ten years? Or heard someone say, "I've always wanted to write a book?" Don't let that be your story with what you know now. No judgment if it's where you're starting (hey, we've all been there!), but here's your wake-up call: it's time to move from dreaming to doing today. Every day you wait is one less day you have to devote to building your own table.

KEEP YOUR PROJECT QUIET UNTIL IT'S READY

One of my personal rules is I don't share what I'm working on until it's 90% done. Why? Because once you spill the beans, people start asking, "How's that book coming along?" and, bam, pressure mounts. What if the book isn't coming along? What if your priorities have shifted?

That doesn't mean you shouldn't start today—quite the opposite. Start now, even if what you're creating feels messy or incomplete. Progress, no matter how small, beats waiting for the "perfect" moment to begin. With a trusted accountability partner, you can approach this goal and potential pitfalls intentionally.

Starting today doesn't mean rushing to share half-baked work. Mediocrity stems from impatience and a lack of consistency. Just as your muscles become stronger the more reps you do over time, stopping your workouts will result in losing your gains. Starting and stopping will reset your gains.

I suggest taking your time to develop your ideas, let your ideas marinate, refine your technical abilities, and listen to the voice of what you're creating. Art is alive. Art has consciousness. Sometimes pieces want to be written but not shared yet. When the time comes to share, you'll be proud of what you've created, knowing that it represents your best foot forward.

ACTIONABLE TIPS TO STAY ON TRACK

1. **Set Realistic Goals**

   Don't start by thinking, "I'll write an 80,000-word novel in two weeks!" when you've never written a page! That's how burnout will happen. Start small and lead with a keen awareness of your strengths and weaknesses. Uncover your process to get it done. Maybe your first goal is 500 words a day or finishing one chapter a month. Progress is progress. Eat the elephant one bite at a time.

2. **Break It Down**

   Speaking of elephants, big projects are overwhelming to create and manage. Break yours into milestones, like:

   ✓ Brainstorm and idea dump
   ✓ Outline key actions in Chapter 1
   ✓ Set a goal of 5,000 words
   ✓ Complete the first draft
   ✓ Celebrate each milestone with a gift!

3. **Plan for Burnout (Because It WILL Happen)**

   Like life, writing isn't all sunshine. There will be days when you feel stuck, tired, or like quitting. Plan for those moments:

   - Take breaks to recharge. Writer's block is normal and passes.
   - Have a "comforting and fun activity" to temporarily replace your writing time.
   - Keep a journal to vent your frustrations—it's still writing!

4. **Prepare for Resistance, Criticism, and Gossip**

   Not everyone will cheer you on as you create and when you share. Some friends or family might not understand. They might even resent the time you're investing in yourself. Our social communities have a huge influence over our personal development and goals, so remember no one else will do this work for you. Some may be there for the applause, but they won't be there for the work.

   Some will criticize, and others might gossip about what you reveal or your skill level. Some may be silent and engage with you about everything else but your work. At the end of the day, though, your work is your proof of perseverance—and no one can ever take that away from you. Ask yourself: does what they think matter more than my sense of self?

*

Finishing a project isn't just about having a book to hold. You're also proving to yourself that you're capable and worthy of immense effort. Writing is a mental, emotional, and even spiritual journey that leaves a permanent imprint—not just on paper, but on your perception of what you're capable of.

When I finished *Views from the Cockpit*, I can't even describe the release I felt. The manuscript had sat under my sofa for months because it felt too heavy to deal with while also being inundated by the monotony of work and paying bills. But once I finished and released it, the weight lifted off my shoulders, and I freed myself from the narrative and the work.

Writing is a mental, emotional, and even spiritual journey that leaves a permanent imprint—not just on paper, but on your perception of what you're

At times, I felt exposed, wondering if I said too much, if people would be mad at me, or shocked to know what I experienced, but I found comfort in knowing that no one could take my words and experience away. My intention wasn't to cause harm, I simply wanted to liberate myself. And writing afforded me that opportunity.

Criticism comes in many forms, and learning to navigate the subjectivity of feedback is just as important as handling outside opinions.

5. **Remember, Writing Is Inherently Subjective**

Navigating conflicting opinions is one of the most challenging parts of developing your writing process.

Writing is human. A heart thing. Expression is unique to each individual and intrinsically subjective. No single assessment, rubric, or review can define your work's true worth—even with the best storyline, the most compelling character arc, and the highest command of grammar. A book can be called *brilliant* by one critic and *trash* by another.

Instead of seeing conflicting feedback as proof that you or your work is flawed and letting those opinions exhaust you, hold tightly to the fact that writing is an art, not a science equation.

Below are a few tips to help.

Learn How to Recognize Subjectivity (Quickly)

Storytelling is powerful because it elicits different reactions from different people. These reactions may be sorrow, elation, rage, sadness, all the emotions we covered in Robert Plutchik's wheel.

Take, for example, the varying professional opinions of my first book, *Views from the Cockpit*:

One reviewer found the pacing too fast:

"I sometimes struggled with the very quick pacing. An enormous number of events, places, and people pass by at great speed."

Another praised the storytelling and prose:

"The author effectively blends memories from his own past with biographical details from his father's storied history. Victory's prose is vivid, clear, and pleasantly descriptive."

Another recommended major revision before publication (to sell me their editorial services):

"You haven't asked my opinion, so I hesitated to outline this for you. I decided it's better for me to be honest. I would suggest you put the release on hold until you have a professional editor revise the manuscript."

Another was deeply moved by my use of language:

"I'm overwhelmed by the gorgeous language in this book. So many stellar descriptions stopped me in my tracks, so that I could turn the phrasing around and around in appreciation."

Four different perspectives—same book. Hmm... Since this was my first project, each opinion made me wonder: who's right? I felt like a success one moment and like an imposter the next. Whose opinion was more credible? Who has more degrees at the end of their name?

Isn't there some objective, industry-wide standard that all authors are reaching toward that ONLY industry folk understand?

Let's answer that question with a question: Which books were once rejected and later became household names?

When it was published, *Moby-Dick* was called "absurd" and a failure—now, it's considered one of the greatest American novels.

The Great Gatsby was dismissed as a "cheap love story" in its time, but today, it's taught in schools worldwide.

Beloved by Toni Morrison was challenged for being "too painful," and "too much trauma," yet it won a Pulitzer Prize and cemented Morrison as an icon.

The best creations throughout history are praised and criticized, revered and dismissed—yet they endure.

Chasing universal approval is so enticing. Even as I write these words, of course I hope that majority of readers find this book useful, engaging, and one-of-a-kind. And when we get that positive reinforcement, it feels great because so much work was involved.

But no work will resonate the same way with everyone. What matters most is responding to the call to action. Output and follow-through are the goals.

Develop a Strong Artistic Brand

The best way to stay grounded in your creative journey is to follow your internal compass. This compass is shaped by your experiences and identity as we've discussed—and your identity is actually your artistic brand.

If you can:

- ✓ Separate your ego from your work by understanding that it serves more than just you.
- ✓ See critiques as inputs rather than verdicts of your worth.
- ✓ Remember that art is rebellion and not meant to please everyone.

...you'll have a much easier time navigating the creative industries, which brings me to my last point.

Publishing (like every other industry) Is Political

Awards, five-star reviews, and accolades reflect taste, timing, cultural moments, industry trends, politics, nepotism, and personal relationships.

- ☞ Some books don't get agents or awards—not because they lack merit, but because they don't align with what judges, critics, or industry leaders value at that moment. If you've ever interviewed for your dream job, knowing you had a strong resume, great personality, and the best references ever, yet still got rejected, you know how this works. The decision often has nothing to do with your skill or talent. In some cases, the decision was made before you got there!
- ☞ Some works are rejected because they don't fit the current trend and can't guarantee money or an audience.

Now, let me be honest—if someone offers me an award, I'm going to take it. And I'll cash the check it comes with! Don't get it twisted: recognition is great, and getting paid for your art is an ideal life. But the point is, awards don't determine your value. If you win one, enjoy it. If you don't, keep writing.

I must remind you that success comes from action, persistence, and determination, not from chasing a version of someone else's accomplishments.

These factors may be barriers and challenging to navigate but they don't define your path.

Write the best work you can. Be open to revision. And don't quit. Your creative identity is yours—no external opinion can take that away.

Persist.

Strength Vs. Weakness Writing Assessment

PAUSE & REFLECT

Imagine your work—a book, a film, a painting, or a performance—receives massive critical acclaim and wins a major award. But somehow you learn that the award was given not because of your talent, but because of political agendas, industry connections, or a desire to fill a quota.

- *Write a scene, essay, or poem exploring your reaction.*
- *Do you accept the award anyway? Do you speak out or stay silent?*
- *Does the recognition change how you see your own work?*
- *What does it mean for success to be "earned" vs. "given"?*
- *Would you rather be respected or rewarded—and can you have both?*

INTERACTIVE CHALLENGES

Ready to start managing your time and discipline? Try these:

- **Set a Timer:** Dedicate a nonnegotiable 30 minutes to writing today (no distractions). When the timer rings, you're done—or keep going if you're in the flow. If you have a laptop, try writing until the battery runs out. Be as persistent as you can and establish a routine. And save your files often if you decide to gamble with a low battery strategy
- **Accountability:** Share your goals with one trusted person who'll cheer you on (not pressure you or compare themselves).
- **Create a Rewards System:** When you hit a milestone, treat yourself! Celebrate finishing one of your milestones with your favorite meal or a guilt-free Netflix binge. Think of writing as a relationship that must be nurtured.

DAILY HABITS CHECKLIST FOR IDENTITY-FOCUSED WRITING

1. Set Dedicated (Nonnegotiable) Writing Time

Choose a time of day when you feel most reflective or energized, even if it's just 5-15 minutes. The consistency of a daily writing habit creates momentum and builds confidence. 100 words soon becomes 1,000 words. 1,000 words becomes 10,000 words and on! And yes, 10,000 can become 100,000.

2. Create a Safe Writing Space

Find or create a space where you feel comfortable expressing yourself without fear of interruption. This can be a desk, your car, a park bench, or an unexpected space. Locate a space that invites honesty and creativity.

3. Begin with a Centering Practice

Take a moment to ground yourself before writing. This could be deep breathing, listening to a favorite song, or closing your eyes to connect with your emotions and intentions. Centering allows you to approach the page with clarity.

4. Use Prompts to Spark Ideas

Start with a prompt or question to guide your writing. You can use prompts we've discussed through the book and spurn them into viable projects or a few ideas below:

How do I feel about my identity in this moment?
What would I say to my younger self right now?

Let these prompts serve as doorways to deeper exploration.

5. Free Write Without Judgment or Expectations

Allow your words to flow freely without worrying about grammar, structure, or how they might be perceived by others. Your writing doesn't need to be technical and perfect—it just needs to be true.

6. Use Reflective Words to Process

Intentionally use reflective words like "realize," "understand," "recognize," or "become aware" in your writing. These words help you bridge the past to the present and articulate moments of growth.

Example: "I recognize now that the hesitation I felt as a child wasn't weakness or being indecisive—it was resilience, a way to survive in a world that wasn't ready for me." Then elaborate on how you feel the world wasn't ready.

7. Explore Emotion Through Story

Choose an emotion or experience and turn it into a short story, poem, or letter. Use tools like Robert Plutchik's *Wheel of Emotions* to explore the nuances of your feelings. Writing about emotions helps you name and process them in meaningful ways. Use a framework or technique we've discussed like re-authoring.

8. Include Your Body in Your Writing

Notice how your body feels as you write. Are there tightnesses in your chest or fluttering in your stomach? Describe these sensations directly or as metaphors in your writing to connect your physical experience with your narrative. What you feel the reader will feel.

9. Reframe Negative Thoughts & Negative Influences

When self-doubt or imposter syndrome creeps in, acknowledge it and reframe it—or "remix"—into something empowering.

Instead of thinking: *"No one will care about my story because it's too insignificant,"* try:

- *"This matters because it's mine! Only I can tell this and there's someone out there waiting for me to tell this story in this way."*

Instead of thinking: *"They made me feel small and insignificant,"* try:

- *"Their attempts to limit me fueled my determination to prove that I'm capable of far more than they imagined!"*

Reframing allows you to push past doubt and maintain momentum.

10. Gratitude for Today, Reflect and Plan for Tomorrow

At the end of your session, take a moment to reflect on what you've written. Acknowledge the act of showing up for yourself, even if your writing feels unfinished. Then, set a small intention for tomorrow's session—whether it's revisiting a memory, using a new prompt, or writing for five more minutes on your narrative idea. Keep planning for tomorrow. You'll quickly discover the days add up!

- ☞ To download a PDF copy of this checklist, visit the Resources page.

CHAPTER 15

WRITER'S BLOCK
WRITING TECHNIQUES

At some point, you'll hit writer's block—it's not *if*, but *when*. And no, it doesn't mean you're a fraud, a failure, or destined to be a cashier at Barnes & Noble reading books instead of writing them. It just means your brain might need a moment to regroup.

I've written six books, and I still have stretches where I feel like I couldn't write a coherent email, let alone a manuscript if you ask me. It's okay if you're uninspired. Creativity isn't a faucet you can turn on at will. There are times when you're just tired, and your brain is waving a tiny white flag, begging for a break.

LET THE STORY MARINATE (LIKE A STEAK)

Have you ever eaten an unseasoned steak? I hope not.

Writing works the same way. You don't just slap words on a page and expect them to be perfect. Good stories need time to marinate. Step away. Do literally *anything else*. Listen to music, go for a walk, binge on a terrible reality show, or take a nap. Let the ideas soak in. When you come back, you may suddenly see the missing piece—the plot hole that needs fixing, the character's motivation that finally makes sense.

> *Creativity isn't a faucet you can turn on at will. There are times when you're just tired, and your brain is waving a tiny white flag, begging for a break.*

I've done this myself—sometimes for a few hours, sometimes weeks, and sometimes months!

I began *Embracing All of Me* in December 2023 as an online course idea. But then, I stepped away—overwhelmed and unmotivated.

Six months later, I returned and realized it wasn't just a course. It needed to be a book, a limited podcast series, and more than that, it was part of a larger movement.

That time away made all the difference. Marination brings clarity, depth, and insights you might never find if you never step back.

So, give your story time. Let it breathe.

And when you return? You might witness something truly magical.

JOURNALING ABOUT YOUR WRITER'S BLOCK

If you don't know what to write, write about not knowing what to write. Sounds ridiculous, but trust me—getting your frustration on the page can shake something loose.

Try writing:

- I don't know what happens next in my story, and it's irritating me.
- My main character is stuck. Maybe I should just make them disappear? Alien abduction? Witness protection?
- Is this even writer's block, or am I just hungry?

You might be surprised to find that writing about writer's block can give you the exact idea you need to overcome it. And often, that raw frustration turns into gold you can use in your actual work.

WRITING BACKWARDS: SKIP TO THE END

Most people write forward—from beginning to end. But if you're stuck, reverse-engineer your way out.

Let's say your character, Marcy, survives something life-changing. You don't know how she gets there, but you do know where she ends up. Instead of flailing in the middle, jump to the final scene:

- Where is she?
- What's changed for her?
- Now, rewind—what happened right before that? And before that? And before *that*?

By writing backward, you create signposts instead of wandering in the dark.

JUMPSTART YOUR BRAIN

If all else fails, try one of these:

1. Make a Soundtrack for Your Story

Music stirs emotions. Build a playlist for your story's mood. What would play in the background of your main character's life? A sad indie song? A chaotic drum solo? A 90s R&B track about *yearning*? The right song might inspire a motivation or goal to get you writing. Studying lyrics can unlock a whole scene, even just a single line.

2. Change How You Write

Do you always type? Try handwriting instead. Do you typically write alone? Write with a partner. Or consider dictating ideas into your phone. This is one of my favorites—especially when ideas appear in my dreams and I wake up *desperate* not to forget them. Speaking your ideas out loud can be surprisingly effective for getting through stuck scenes.

Bonus trick: Have a document reader or Google Translate read your passage back to you. Hearing it aloud often reveals awkward phrasing, missing details, or fresh angles you wouldn't catch otherwise.

3. Find a Random Image & Describe It

Go on a treasure hunt. Google your character's name. What colors and images come up? Browse Pinterest or photography websites. Pick an image that intrigues you, and write about it:

- *Who does it belong to?*

- What's happening in this moment?
- How does it connect to your story?

You might accidentally create a new plot twist.

4. Write a Letter to Your Character

Ask them about their desires, their fears, and what they think of *you* as a writer. Then, write a letter from them back to you. This could either lead to a breakthrough or leave you feeling personally attacked.

5. Use the "What If?" Method

Take your current scene and **break it apart** by asking "What if?" five times. Here are some ideas.

- What if my character made the absolute worst decision possible?
- What if a minor background character suddenly became the key to everything?
- What if the setting changed—and the story is now set in space, the 1800s, underwater, a reality show?
- What if the biggest problem in the story was actually a misunderstanding?
- What if I threw in a totally unexpected element—like a secret letter, a missing memory, or a talking parrot with gossip on everyone?

Even if the idea is ridiculous, that's the point—it shakes things loose to find something usable. What if the "What if?" turns out to be the missing piece?

VOLUNTEER

Volunteering may seem like an unexpected solution to writer's block, but it can disrupt creative stagnation by shifting focus away from internal pressure and mind chatter toward real-world connection. Engaging with others through service offers fresh perspectives and untold stories, reigniting inspiration in ways isolation cannot. The look of someone's eyes, the way they laugh, and how they got into the situation they are in can serve as inspiration.

Acts of service can also help quiet self-doubt by fostering presence and deepening our awareness of the immediate world around us. It's a powerful reminder that our words and ideas hold value beyond the page. Simply stepping outside of yourself is all you need to find your way back.

> *Acts of service can also help quiet self-doubt by fostering presence and deepening our awareness of the immediate world around us.*

Writer's block happens to everyone, and it's 100% normal. The best thing you can do is step back, breathe, and trust that the ideas will return when they're ready.

Creativity is honest, but sometimes it can benefit from a break. When you let go of the pressure to force words, they often find their way back, just like the best things in life always seem to.

CHAPTER 16
BUILDING AN ALL-STAR TEAM
WRITING TECHNIQUES

"Only recently have I realized that being different is not something you want to hide or squelch or suppress."
– Amy Gerstler, Poet

A wise author builds their best piece with the support of a talented and committed team. *Committed* is key here because talent alone doesn't ensure follow-through. You need accountability, passion, and dedication to keep the project moving forward, especially when your energy wanes. You need people who "get it."

Have you ever seen a terrible movie and thought, HOW. THE. HELL. DID. THIS. GET. MADE? It's not just that art is subjective and people have different opinions; it's also about what actions were taken to create it. Your jaw will drop lower when you see the multi-million dollar budget they were given.

The people behind the film had strong convictions and were committed to work hard—step by step—to achieve their finished product. In the end, someone who takes consistent action will go further more than someone who's more talented but paralyzed by doubt.

If you're working alone or with a small team, it may feel like you're held to an unrealistic standard. Finishing your project may feel unattainable because you believe you can't compete with large publishers. And you're right. While their budget might be a million, ours might only be one hundred. It's not fair. It's not fair that not only do we have to sacrifice or compromise our authenticity to get our work published, but we also don't have a team with a large budget and the opportunities that come with more cash.

Have you ever seen a terrible movie and thought, HOW. THE. HELL. DID. THIS. GET. MADE? It's not just that art is subjective and people have different opinions; it's also about what actions were taken to create it.

Like navigating oppression, we must decide how we respond to this reality. Will you choose to move forward baby step by baby step to build your own victory? Can you take a moment to assess what you can do?

Traditional publishing is one avenue, but are you open to an independent publisher, hybrid publishing, or self-publishing as alternatives? Will you stay standing when the odds are stacked, when gatekeepers scoff, and when doubt whispers that you'll never measure up? Only the strong survive.

Our journeys are not the same, and while we all reach for the same dreams, only a few will have a chance to experience them. But we must reach. Greatness isn't built overnight, and success isn't just for the chosen few—it's for those who believe in themselves and find inspiration in their environment because of it.

It's more than writing a book or finishing a project. Investing in action also means evolving interpersonally, strengthening relationships, and holding yourself accountable.

Every step you take toward your creative goal—any goal—every conversation where you reveal your dreams, and every collaboration where you invite others to join you is an act of self-advocacy. By default, it's also an act of rebellion against all the invisible forces holding us down.

What is the difference between a creative with a 30-year career and someone who stalls out at the starting line? Some may argue talent, but I believe it's commitment. It's the willingness to do the work—scared, tired, bored, and filled with doubt. A committed person doesn't let their ego—or their fear—prevent them from taking another step. They reach for tomorrow, one action at a time.

YOUR SUPPORT TEAM A CIRCLE OF STRENGTH

To get your project done, you'll need an editor, a designer for both exterior and interior elements (this can sometimes be the same person), a proofreader, and a publisher or platform to bring your work to the world. While free resources like Grammarly or AI tools can help with drafting and outlining, they can't replace another set of human eyes. Another significant factor to consider is that your identity-focused writing is also your brand as a writer.

Every step you take toward your creative goal—any goal—every conversation where you reveal your dreams, and every collaboration where you invite others to join you is an act of self-advocacy.

Think about whether you want your work to be represented publicly. Not only your words and your perspective but also your professionalism and attention to detail. Editors and designers, if you can afford them, offer feedback which can enrich your work, spotting blind spots you may have missed and helping ensure your intention translates, and trimming unnecessary content.

Seek out collaborators who challenge you, encourage your strengths, and fill in skill gaps. You can only do so much. In writing this book, the "CTRL F" function became my best friend. I sometimes use the same concept or repeat myself and inadvertently create distracting filler language. By using CTRL F, I can search the frequency of certain words and phrases. Instead of doing this alone, building a team can help get the job done and create a network of people who elevate you and reduce your stress.

Don't let your ego prevent you from accepting help or constructive feedback. More eyes on your work can mean more opportunities and also increase your exposure to criticism and fear, like we talked about earlier with how the brain reacts to seeing a spider.

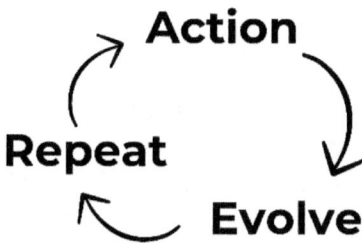

The work is proof of your commitment—both to the project and yourself. The more you engage with your goals, the more confidence you build.

TIPS FOR CHOOSING AN EDITOR(S)

As I already said, an editor plays a crucial role in the development of your book. Here are some tips on choosing one:

- First, determine what kind of an edit you require: concept and developmental editing (fleshing out ideas, brainstorming directions), copy editing (to fix grammar and punctuation issues), or beta reading (to react as a reader would).

- Be flexible as you tell the editor your expectations.
- Communicate your intention to the editor to see if they are familiar with your goals. A professional editor will likely ask to see the piece, confirm the word count, or gather other specifics before agreeing to the job.
    - For example, you don't want to hire a textbook editor to edit your poetry!
- A word of caution: since editors are not personally invested in your work, their recommendations to cut, omit, and alter may feel personal and trigger your ego as a new writer.
- Negotiate the price, but be careful not to undermine their contribution. This will bite you in the butt if you expect someone to fix everything but are not willing to pay the appropriate price. Don't give anyone on your team a reason to resent you while working on your life's work!
- Ask yourself what level of copyediting you actually require. This assessment should be based on your personal strengths and where you need the most support.
    - **Light:** Fixing grammar, punctuation, and minor clarity issues. ($)
    - **Medium:** Grammar, sentence flow, and some restructuring for readability. ($$)
    - **Heavy:** Deep edits on clarity, conciseness, word choice, and flow while keeping your voice intact. ($$$)
- Ask yourself if there are any sections you want special attention to, such as clarity, transitions, or tone.

- Clarify if you want your editor to track changes with suggested edits or apply them directly. I prefer the option to review the changes and any notes in case I wrote something a certain way intentionally.

TIPS FOR FINDING A WRITER'S COMMUNITY

Writing can seem like a lonely job, but it doesn't really have to be that way. If you're a new writer, or even a seasoned one, you can find friends in the writing community. These can't be random people you meet in "internet streets."

They must be people who share the same likes, values, and writing styles. Use discernment here; everyone who supports your writing and career may not necessarily identify like you do. Additionally, everyone who identifies like you may not support your writing and career. Make sure the community you build around you is one that you can trust.

I've found writer's communities on Facebook and Medium. As you search for the ideal group for you, associate with people who value personal freedom and have walked similar paths or are pursuing similar goals or higher goals. You want to reach up. Accomplished people are typically not threatened by your aspirations.

"Real transformation requires real honesty.
If you want to move forward—get real with yourself."

— Bryant McGill, Activist

REMINDERS

- Remember, you can't improve on what you haven't attempted to do, so why not start today? Never forget that someone out there needs your story the way you've written it. There are almost ten billion people in the world. It may feel like you're alone, but you're not. We're so fortunate to live in the digital era where information and community are at our fingertips along with voice command.

- There is still a child in you. There is a child in each of us that never dies. What would your life look like if you were to tap into that childhood joy for one minute? How about an hour? A day? A week? A year? A decade? The rest of your life? Can you imagine?

- Consider using Sunday as a rest day. Always remember to take a break, rest, and focus all your energy on yourself. You need the rest. Pick a single day every weekend and take time to meditate, travel, soak in a spa, get a deep tissue massage, and revitalize your mind. Back when I had a regular job, I was on a weekly massage rotation. Now, not so much! Do what you can afford and do something that makes you feel good.

- You may wake up and regret being vulnerable. You may ask yourself, "Did I write too much?" "Did I say too much?" It's key for you to align your intention. You must be mindful of your choices, and this book has hopefully helped you become more aware. Think of vulnerability as stretching. A good stretch will improve your overall workout. If you overstretch, you'll cause harm or injury. The goal is improvement.

- If you're looking for a way to share your writing tonight, online platforms offer instant access to an audience. Sites like Medium, Substack, WordPress, CreateSpace, and Blogger allow new writers to publish their work for free—blogs, essays, poetry, or personal reflections.

One of the best parts? Direct connection with readers. Unlike traditional publishing, where feedback can be slow (or nonexistent), online publishing allows immediate engagement—people can comment, share, and spark conversations, whether they resonate with your words or challenge them from a different perspective.

I started publishing on Medium years ago, sharing thoughts and personal essays on mental health, race, religion, and sexuality. Over time, my audience grew, and in 2024, I led my first Medium Day conference session, "Writing Through the Storm." What started as small, self-published pieces became a speaking opportunity to talk about what I love in front of strangers.

For new writers, these platforms serve as a training ground and a launchpad—a place to experiment, develop your author voice and brand, and build a readership without waiting for permission. The key? Begin. Share. Rinse. Repeat.

CHAPTER 17
FINAL THOUGHTS

"There are years that ask questions and years that answer."
– Zora Neale Hurston

I want to close our time together with an inspiring real-life example that ties together *Embracing All of Me* and the power of identity-focused writing in the most resonant way.

DIANA ATHILL
A LIFE OF RETURNING TO HERSELF

Diana Athill was born in Norfolk, England, in 1917. She spent most of her life as an editor at André Deutsch, shaping the voices of authors like Margaret Atwood, Jean Rhys, and V.S. Naipaul. Working tirelessly behind the scenes, she brought countless stories to life, but it wasn't until her nineties that she fully stepped into her own spotlight.

At 91 years old, Athill published *Somewhere Towards the End* (2008), a memoir exploring love, sex, regret, and the realities of a body in decline—topics women of her generation were often expected to avoid. The book won the Costa Biography Award and catapulted her to international fame. Practically overnight, she was giving interviews, appearing on television, and being celebrated for work that had taken a lifetime to produce.

But we know that amazing things don't happen overnight. And we know that *Somewhere Towards the End* was not her first book. So what caused her sudden success?

Some might call her a "late bloomer," but that would misrepresent the decades of groundwork Athill laid—within herself and for others, quietly and publicly. She didn't "arrive" at 91, and she wasn't living in the shadows for most of her life. She arrived the moment she decided she was worthy—that she mattered.

> She didn't "arrive" at 91, and she wasn't living in the shadows for most of her life. She arrived the moment she decided she was worthy—that she mattered.

Athill, like most of us, had been unfolding herself over the decades, choosing again and again, little by little, to embrace and embody her inner light—the strengths and identities that endured. Imagine if she had stopped at 31, 41, 61, or even 81.

Surely, there were years—or even decades—when she felt uninspired. But it's the returning, the act of coming back to the project or truth and that "inner voice" that endures.

In a 2010 interview with *The Guardian*, she explained: "If there's something on my mind and it won't go away, then I write about it. I only write when I have to."

This is the inescapable truth about embracing all of you:

- It is not one moment of arrival.

- It is not a single breakthrough project.
- It is a commitment—to strengthening, sharpening, and returning to yourself day by day, year by year.

It is the act of choosing to reach for tomorrow, through decades of joy and sorrow, knowing that each word, each story, each act of self-expression is another step forward.

Athill's journey reminds us that self-expression has no expiration date—but it takes work. The life we build, word by word, story by story, is what ultimately defines us.

A FINAL WORD FOR MY BI+ BROS

And for my Bi+ men—my beautiful bisexual+, pansexual, fluid, nonconforming, omnisexual, no-labeling brothers. You, who are loyal friends, dedicated fathers, uncles, brothers, intentional lovers, and servant leaders...

They *will* rewrite us. Deny us. Pathologize us. Bigotry and bias will persist in collective memory and the preservation of records. Some will fall on the sword to claim we don't exist.

The goalpost will move. We will be gaslit. A century from now, they may call us something else entirely. But hear me *(especially those in the back)*: no one speaks for you. No one holds the pen except for you.

Will you break under the weight or stand armored in truth and action, tracing the footprints of those who've climbed this mountain before you?

What will you name and claim as your own? What will you reject?

Final Thoughts

Diana Athill once wrote,

"*Look! Why want anything more than what is.*"

So—what will you say?

You don't have to be perfect. You don't have to have all the answers. Do what you can. What you *can* is enough.

The world won't hand us acknowledgment. We gotta take it. The world won't hand us respect. We gotta create it. The world won't hand us visibility. We have to demand it and be it.

And when we do, we don't just change ourselves. We shift the storyline of what it means to be bi+ and proud.

There are nearly ten billion people in the world. Millions speak your language. Your tribe is out there. You were never alone in this.

If this lit a fire in you, don't let it burn out. Speak. Write. Post. Say the thing you once needed to hear. Someone out there is waiting for it.

When you do, use #EmbracingAllOfMe and remember:

My Story. My Terms. OUR POWER. Period!

EMBRACING ALL OF ME
A MANTRA

I stand,
a maelstrom of self-awareness and strength.

I have dived into the realms of knowledge,
unraveled the labyrinth of my identity,
seeking to understand how
I've been tethered to the world around me.

I stand,
grounded,
a pillar through storms awaiting the sun.

I wield the power of language,
my voice,
my truth—
unflinchingly.

I see through the smoke and mirrors
I am not committed to being defeated
I am committed to my liberation.

I seek new heights,
embracing every hue of my being.
I hold every nuance,
every puzzle piece,
every paradox,
every longing
with grace.

I am a beacon of transformation—
with nothing to prove,
nothing to defend.
I will no longer be gaslit

Final Thoughts

by those who have done no work,
those who offer no reciprocity.
I decide how deep to let people in.

My narrative weaves through history's fabric.
I cannot be erased.
Each emotion pulses through me—
molding me,
reminding me:
I am alive.
I am human.
I am real.

Where I once cried,
I stand triumphant.
Grateful.
Whole.

I forgive myself for
judgements undue to me.

And on this odyssey of self-discovery,
I am unshackled.
I roam free
of borrowed perspectives.

I am safe in my body.
I engage with others' thoughts, ideas, and dreams—
but I remain unbound.

I put on my oxygen mask first.
I see my reflection first.

Nothing anyone can do,
say,
think,

or dream
can deter me from my progress.

In that, I choose to nourish all my identities.
I hold them with clarity,
with patience,
becoming a prototype of resilience.

I have accepted not just my light,
but my shadows
and how they've have shaped me,
taught me the profound beauty of myself.

Here, I stand:
unbroken,
unwavering,
limitless,
resilient beyond measure.

I accept every tear,
every scar,
every smile,
every muscle.

And in doing so,
I embrace all of me.
I see all of me.

I am worthy.
I am here.

Written by Ross Victory

SOURCES

Centers for Disease Control and Prevention (CDC). (2021). *Adverse Childhood Experiences (ACEs) reported by U.S. adults.* National Center for Injury Prevention and Control.

Substance Abuse and Mental Health Services Administration (SAMHSA). (2022). *Trauma and mental health statistics in the U.S.* U.S. Department of Health and Human Services.

Association for Psychological Science. (2013). *Expressive writing and its impact on mental health.* Psychological Science.

Jung, C. G. (1953-1979). *The Collected Works of C.G. Jung.* Princeton University Press.

Johnson, M. J., Mimiaga, M. J., & Bradford, J. B. (2008). *Health care issues among lesbian, gay, bisexual, and transgender individuals.* Annals of the New York Academy of Sciences, 1136(1), 205-221.

Williams, W. L. (1986). *The Spirit and the Flesh: Sexual Diversity in American Indian Culture.* Beacon Press.

Van der Kolk, B. (2014). *The Body Keeps the Score: Brain, Mind, and Body in the Healing of Trauma.* Viking Press.

Pew Research Center. (2013). *Visibility and stigma of bisexual adults in the U.S.* Pew Research Center: Social & Demographic Trends.

BiNet USA. (1999). *History of the bisexual movement and activism in the U.S.* BiNet USA archives.

HBO. (2000, July 9). *Sex and the City, Season 3, Episode 4: "Boy, Girl, Boy, Girl...".*

Yoshino, K. (2006). *Covering: The Hidden Assault on Our Civil Rights.* Random House.

Muñoz, J. E. (1999). *Disidentifications: Queers of Color and the Performance of Politics.* University of Minnesota Press.

Shelley, Mary. (1818). *Frankenstein; or, The Modern Prometheus.* Lackington, Hughes, Harding, Mavor & Jones.

Romero, George A. (Director). (1968). *Night of the Living Dead.* Image Ten.

King, Stephen. (1983). *Christine.* Viking Press.

Onoda, Hiroo. (1974). *No Surrender: My Thirty-Year War.* Kodansha International.

Ginzburg, Eugenia. (1967). *Journey into the Whirlwind.* Harcourt Brace & Company.

Maya Angelou. (1974). *Gather Together in My Name.* Random House.

The Autobiography of Malcolm X as told to Alex Haley. (1965). Grove Press.

Bridget "Biddy" Mason: Pioneer Entrepreneur and Philanthropist. California African American Museum.

Plato. (c. 385 BCE). *Symposium.*

Green, P. (2013). *Alexander the Great and the Hellenistic Age.* Modern Library.

Hubbard, T. K. (2003). *Homosexuality in Greece and Rome: A Sourcebook of Basic Documents.* University of California Press.

Murray, S. O., & Roscoe, W. (1998). *Boy-Wives and Female Husbands: Studies of African Homosexualities.* Palgrave Macmillan.

Salmón, E. (2012). *Eating the Landscape: American Indian Stories of Food, Identity, and Resilience.* University of Arizona Press.

Silverblatt, I. (1987). *Moon, Sun, and Witches: Gender Ideologies and Class in Inca and Colonial Peru.* Princeton University Press.

ACKNOWLEDGMENTS

To Will, whose cover design didn't just meet the moment—it met me at the intersection of vision and magic. To every editor on the editor page who endured my comma sprees and late-night rewrites with saint-like patience, thank you. To my Bi+ community and contributors, especially my Black bisexual brothers—you are balm, brilliance, and backbone. Thank you for allowing us to witness your resilience and talent. To my ancestors, thank you for whispering courage into my bones and ambition into my chest. Thank you for giving me the gift of curiosity. And finally, to myself—for not quitting, for showing up, for going to therapy, for doing the work, and for believing that this project was worth the follow through.

You amaze me daily!

OTHER BOOKS BY THE AUTHOR

Views from the Cockpit: The Journey of a Son (2019)
A personal memoir of loss, reconciliation, and the enduring bond between father and son.

Panorama (2020)
A vivid exploration of human connections through memoir and societal critique.

Egg (2020)
A surreal and horror short story that cracks open questions of fertility and family.

Father & Sun (2020)
A holiday novella-length short story on legacy, love, and the echoes we leave behind, and their connectedness to the universe.

Grandpa's Cabin Series (Book 1) (2023)
A horror series exploring the life and times of Bernie Crenshaw and this legacy as a geneticist and grandfather.

Borderland: Poetry and Words from the Intersection of Masculinity, Race, Bisexuality, and Grief (2024)
A genre-bending collection that embraces the beauty of complexity and the power of truth-telling.

RESOURCES PAGE

Free worksheets, affirmations, checklists, all writing prompts, all pause and reflect activities, and more!

https://rossvictory.com/embracingresources

LISTEN TO THE PODCAST

Real stories. Honest reflection. Our voices amplified.

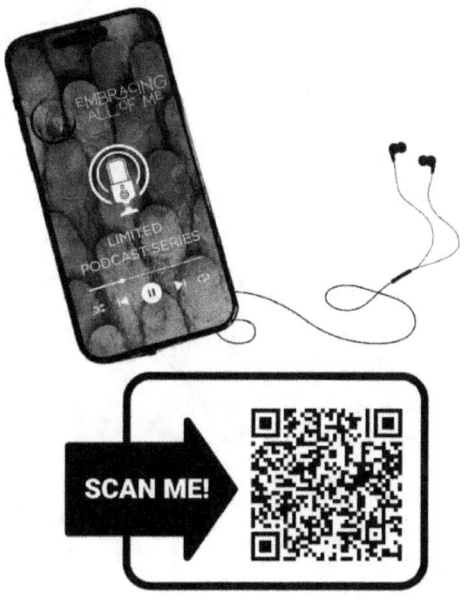

SUGGESTED READING

ON IDENTITY

The Mastery of Self: A Toltec Guide to Personal Freedom by Don Miguel Ruiz, Jr.

- A guide that blends Toltec wisdom with modern self-awareness, teaching readers how to break free from societal conditioning and live authentically.

The Body Keeps the Score by Bessel van der Kolk, M.D.

- This book explores how trauma is stored in the body and how creative practices like writing can aid in processing it.

Writing Down the Bones: Freeing the Writer Within by Natalie Goldberg

- A classic guide to writing with authenticity, Goldberg offers meditative and intuitive techniques to explore identity and creative expression. It's perfect for beginners looking to connect writing with self-discovery.

Final Thoughts

ON BISEXUALITY

Rec-og-nize: The Voices of Bisexual Men: An Anthology, Edited by Robyn Ochs and H. Sharif Williams

- A powerful collection of personal essays that amplifies the diverse experiences of bisexual men, challenging stereotypes and fostering visibility.

Dear Bi Men by J.R. Yussuf

- A heartfelt and affirming letter-style book that speaks directly to bisexual men, offering support, validation, and guidance in navigating identity and relationships.

Married Bisexual Men: Stories of Relationships, Acceptance, and Authenticity by Robert Brooks Cohen

- A thought-provoking exploration of the lives of married bisexual men, examining their relationships, identities, and the complexities of love and desire.

Bisexual Men Speak by Vaneet Mehta

- A compelling collection of real-life stories from bisexual men, shedding light on their struggles, triumphs, and the need for greater acceptance in society.

ON FEAR AND IMAGINATION

Big Magic: Creative Living Beyond Fear by Elizabeth Gilbert

- This book dives into the fears that hold writers back and how to embrace creativity with courage.

On Writing: A Memoir of the Craft by Stephen King

- Part memoir, part masterclass, King offers both technical advice and personal insights on overcoming fear and embracing imagination. A must-read for blending craft with personal experience.

ON GRAMMAR AND WRITING TECHNIQUES

The Right to Write: An Invitation and Initiation into the Writing Life (Artist's Way) by Julia Cameron

- A practical guide that encourages writers of all levels to embrace creativity, overcome self-doubt, and view writing as a natural, joyful practice.

The Elements of Style by William Strunk Jr. and E.B. White

- This concise and accessible guide to grammar and style is perfect for writers who want to sharpen their technical skills without getting bogged down.

Dreyer's English: An Utterly Correct Guide to Clarity and Style by Benjamin Dreyer

- With humor and practicality, Dreyer offers advice on grammar, punctuation, and style, making technical writing fun and approachable.

ON THE ROLE OF AI IN WRITING

AI 2041: Ten Visions for Our Future by Kai-Fu Lee and Chen Qiufan

- While not directly about creative writing, this book explores the future of AI and creativity, offering insight into how AI might shape storytelling and identity-focused writing in years to come.

ABOUT THE AUTHOR

Ross Victory is an award-winning author, poet, music artist, former English teacher, and entrepreneur—blending storytelling and advocacy across genres and formats to explore identity and promote personal transformation.

www.ingramcontent.com/pod-product-compliance
Lightning Source LLC
LaVergne TN
LVHW021801060526
838201LV00058B/3189